When Life Is the Pits

In **When Life Is the Pits,** Robert Reccord provides lessons in abundant living from the life of Joseph: The Joseph presented here is not some storybook character, but a real man who faced disappointments, betrayal, hardships, false accusations, and pressing temptations. Yet Joseph continually triumphed over oppressing circumstances by practicing perseverance, service, and obedience. As a result, his life was richly blessed by the God he served so faithfully. Robert Reccord gives a victorious picture of what life can be when you're living in a personal relationship with God through Christ, empowered by the Holy Spirit. Thoroughly practical, **When Life Is the Pits** gives you refreshing insight for responding positively to life's adverse circumstances.

When Life Is the Pits

A Bible Study On the Life of Joseph

ROBERT E. RECCORD

Foreword by LEIGHTON FORD

Fleming H. Revell Company
Old Tappan, New Jersey

Library of Congress Cataloging-in-Publication Data

Reccord, Robert E.
    When life is the pits.

    Bibliography: p.
    1. Christian life 1960–   . 2. Consolation.
3. Success. I. Title.
BV4501.2.R38   1987   248.8'6   87-14707
ISBN 0-8007-5254-6

Copyright © 1987 by Dr. Robert E. Reccord
Published by the Fleming H. Revell Company
Old Tappan, New Jersey 07675
Printed in the United States of America

With deep affection and appreciation, I dedicate this volume

TO Eck and Ruth Reccord—parents who gave me the
opportunities and support to grow up
living life to the maximum

and

TO Cheryl, my wife, who has been God's gift of love
and encouragement to me. She has shown me what
living life to the maximum as an adult is all about.
Without her, this all would have been impossible.

I thank my God every time I remember you. In all my
prayers for all of you, I always pray with joy because of your
partnership in the gospel from the first day until now.

Philippians 1:3–5

Contents

Contents

Foreword

Suppose you were the only believer in your school or office, your city, your entire country. What do you think God would want you to do and to be? The story of Joseph is the story of a man in just such a position, of God's call and providence, and how that affected his faith and life-style. Joseph's story is not unusual. Today there are millions of believers who are in almost exactly the same situation. The gospel they sometimes hear—"trust God and you will have health, wealth, success, and no problems"—just doesn't ring true. I think of the businessman with whom I shared a conversation on a recent flight. When he turned his life over to Christ some years ago, it led to a new life-style in the market-place. His motivation to serve his company and his effectiveness actually went up. But eventually, because he made others uncomfortable, he lost his job.

For all of us who struggle with the call to be godly in what is often an ungodly world, my friend Bob Reccord has done a signal service. His book about Joseph bridges the two worlds of Egypt in Joseph's day and our dilemmas in the present day. Using biblical material and his own experience and reading, Bob Reccord helps us to see how God can work in our own lives as He did in Joseph's. Here we see Joseph not as a far-off romantic, but a real man in a real world who faced, as we do, disappointments, betrayal, hardships, false accusations, and pressing temptations.

I like Bob's book because it is biblical, it is practical, it is honest (not promising easy solutions to hard problems), and it gives a feeling of identity. The author comes across not as an expert spouting pious advice, but a fellow journeyman in the pilgrimage of life, sharing his insights. Part of the reason is that Bob has lived in two worlds—the real world of the church where he has been a pastor, helping real people with real problems, and the real world of business where Sunday talk has to be translated into Monday-through-Friday walk.

People from all walks of life will find this book helpful. I thank Bob Reccord for it and hope this is only the first of many he will write.

LEIGHTON FORD

Introduction

LIFE CAN BE THE PITS

Things had been idyllic. You had been so comfortable in your warm and insulated environment. Now all that had suddenly turned topsy-turvy.

It all started when you began to feel pressure. Before you knew what was happening, you were being hurled through a tunnellike passage. What had been a secure, fully equipped hideaway was abruptly replaced by a blinding white light and a number of animated voices.

As if that wasn't enough, your next sensation was that of a firm hand lambasting your derriere. And this was a *welcome* to the world!

Immediately you had that "the cards are stacked against me" sensation. You knew it would require a gladiatorial stand just to survive this experience.

Unfortunately it didn't stop there. You were taken home from the hospital and immediately put on display. You felt like one of the monkeys at the zoo. (You probably resembled them as well.) Those silly giants called adults came to peer over your crib, making the most ridiculous sounds you had ever heard. *If that's the way they talk, how do they manage to understand each other?* you thought.

Surely things would improve with time. But alas . . . you next found yourself imprisoned in some silly contraption called a playpen. How preposterous! Anyone with sense would know that your life-style was being cramped. How could you conquer the world beyond if you were left to peer mournfully out between the bars? Whenever you let your desires for freedom be known and cried for a savior, those silly adults always misinterpreted. They brought you food or attempted to hold you and, at times, changed your diaper—or sometimes simply ignored you. What an educational process it would be for you to get them trained properly.

As you grew, it was off to new and exciting frontiers. School was the next bastion to be assailed. There were new friends and toys. You set out determined to make your niche in this new sociological grouping. Some kids wanted to be nurses, firemen, or policemen. Not you. You had bigger aspirations. King of the world would do nicely, thank you.

Directly in your way to the ascendancy over your new class, however, was a roadblock. It was called "teacher." She just did not understand your goals! What was this nonsense she was espousing about how much fun it was to share toys? Boy, she sure didn't have the inside track on management through intimidation.

What's more, just about the time you were getting your second wind, she was telling you to lie down on your mat for a nap! She definitely had not been schooled in the fine art of winning friends and influencing people.

The odds against you were stacking higher and higher. About the fifth grade it happened. It came out of nowhere. You had been bitten before you even knew what was happening. Love had exploded in your heart. The lucky recipient of your affections was—who else—your teacher. Never had someone so captivated your thoughts and imagination. You tried to get to school early and didn't mind getting in trouble if it meant staying after school with him or her.

Just when you were convinced that your teacher would wait for you to get out of school to get married, it happened. It was accidental, of course. You were caught by surprise. After school you were walking through the parking lot on your way home when you saw your teacher walk over to a waiting car. She got in and—horrors—kissed the person who had been waiting! Your heart shattered into a million pieces.

Finally, as the years passed, dating age arrived. Your heart had been captured again—this time by someone your own age. (You can never trust those "older" heartthrobs anyway.) The evening of your first date arrived. You started getting ready at 3:00 P.M.—your date wasn't until 7:30. Everything was ready when you glanced into the mirror for the fortieth time. You hadn't noticed it before. But, big as life, there it was. On the end of your nose. A *pimple*. Try as you might, you could not get rid of it. Even Mom's best makeup would not cover the monstrosity. Foiled again.

So it goes through life. Our age changes. Circumstances vary. But more than once, we all feel as though the odds are against us and life is getting to be the pits. Perhaps that's why so many of us can well identify with Joseph in the Old Testament. His life went from the pinnacle to the pit and back up to the pinnacle again. Only for a rare minority does life progress on a continuous comfortable plateau. Each of us experiences the heights and the depths of life. The real question becomes, "How do we deal with them?" Joseph walks out of the pages of the Old Testament as an exemplary model. Most of us can well identify with him since he was never a preacher-type or a hired holy man. Instead he starts out in a family business, struggles through betrayal and rejection by his siblings, becomes the executive manager of an estate, is falsely accused and imprisoned, only to rise from the ashes to become the prominent leader and political figure of his day. This fellow really knew what life was about!

Though many of us will never experience quite the extremes of heights and depths which Joseph lived through, we are well able to identify with the emotions and struggles with which he had to deal. To read his life is akin to reading the daily newspaper. Investigating his false accusation is reminiscent of a "60 Minutes" exposé. To see him jump onto the stage as a leader while seeming to come out of nowhere reminds us of Jimmy Carter's amazing ascension to the presidency. Most amazing of all, the family life in which Joseph was raised sounds strikingly similar to the chaotic home life of millions in our time.

"But what," you are probably asking, "does Joseph have to do with today?" I'm glad you asked that question. Scripture says that the Old Testament was written to give us a picture of what life can be when living in a personal relationship with God through Christ. God's Word says, "For everything that was written in the past was written to teach us, so that through endurance and the encouragement of the Scriptures we might have hope" (Romans 15:4). As if to nail down the point, the Bible reiterates in 1 Corinthians 10:11, "These things happened to them as examples and were written down as warnings for us, on whom the fulfillment of the ages has come." Joseph did not have the privilege of living, as we do, in the age of grace. When the Holy Spirit was active in the day of Joseph, He worked externally in the lives of people. The Spirit would endue people with power and characteristics that would enable them to have dynamic impact. Today we live in a new age. Rather than working externally, the Holy Spirit works internally. The Bible indicates that He comes to indwell in our lives and take up residence. This divine inhabitation is contingent upon a personal relationship with Jesus Christ. Therefore, Joseph serves as a "prefillment" of what the empowered Christian life can be.[1]

Journey with me back into time to look at the life of this outstanding man. You will find insights that will aid you in living a truly successful life. You will walk with him through the dilemmas of our day, gleaning principles which will greatly enhance both your life and that of your family. You will walk with him through his family life, his personal struggles, and his moments of success.

I challenge you to open your mind to the principles found in God's Word for abundant living. As you read, don't allow your eyes merely to race across the words, but instead ask God's Holy Spirit to speak to you. Be open to evaluate where you are. Perhaps you are in the pits and need to get out. On the other hand, perhaps you are at the pinnacle and need to avoid the pits. Maybe you are just in between and not sure where you are but feel as though you have both feet firmly planted in midair. I challenge you to take these maxims and apply them to your life. They will truly become maxims for maximum living.

When
Life Is
the Pits

1

Overcoming a Weak Foundation

> ### MAXIM:
> A cracked foundation can be filled with the mortar of godly attitudes.

He grew up in a small river town hidden away on a Midwest riverbank. The town was best known to river pirates and those who walked on the wild side. Shawneetown, Illinois, was not the most conducive place in the world to start a new life.

To complicate matters further, his young mother had no desire to be tied down by an infant. The father acted as though the child did not exist. He denied any knowledge of his fatherhood. Looking for a way out, the young mother gave the child to her mother and stepfather. What seemed already to be a senseless tragedy deepened when the grandmother died while the child was still very young. Thus it was to an alcoholic stepgrandfather that he now became accountable. *Accountable* was rather a useless word as the stepgrandfather was by no means a shining example of guardianship.

With the stepgrandfather often intoxicated, the young man was left to fend for himself. Meals were often found in other people's garbage or made from corn and other grains left in the barns of surrounding farms. Add to these circumstances the name *Estel* and the young man was in a no-win situation. Other boys constantly made fun of his name, intimating that he had a less-than-macho character. In reaction he lashed out in an attempt to defend himself and what little character he felt he possessed. This attitude led to numerous fights and association with the wrong crowd.

It wasn't long before fights and gang-type activities were commonplace. He quickly became both athletic and tough in a desperate attempt merely to defend himself against a world that seemed to be so cruel. Before he knew it he found himself in a gang fight in which another youth unexpectedly pulled a knife. With a flash of a hand quicker than the eye, the knife was sunk home deep into his leg. He tumbled to the ground. When the fighting cleared, a few whose consciences wouldn't let them leave him lying there, picked him up and carried him to the hospital. The wound had come close to severing a major artery.

It wasn't until he reached young adulthood that he met a person who changed his life. That person was my mother. The young man was my father. It was through Christian faith held by this special lady and love that kept on giving that my father's life was transformed. He overcame the weak foundation of his early life to become, at least in my eyes, an outstanding man.

So it is in the lives of many. Life is begun in less than ideal circumstances. Often it would seem that these circumstances are enough to destroy or at least cripple healthy development. Yet time and time again brave souls rise above a foundation that was crumbling. Leonardo da Vinci was an illegitimate child. J. S. Bach was an orphan. Camus, Edgar Allen Poe, Dante, Tolstoy, Voltaire, and Jean Jacques Rousseau all came from homes that were crumbling.

You remember the tragic-triumphant story of Helen Keller. Few realize, however, the background of her tutor, Anne Sullivan. As a young girl she had been locked in a mental institution cell and proclaimed mentally disturbed. She had been labeled "hopelessly" insane. Had it not been for an elderly nurse whose heart went out to Anne and who began gradually to give her little pieces of her lunch, she possibly could have rotted her life away in the institution. Gradually, however, she changed from living like an animal to responding to the food.

Doctors soon began to notice a change occurring in the young girl. In a short time she was moved upstairs and given professional treatment. After she had overcome her difficulties she stayed on at the institution helping other patients come out of their disturbed states. And this was all done before she even met Helen Keller.

Paul Tournier, the well-known physician and counselor, has written a book dealing with such incidences. In *Creative Suffering*, Tournier proposed that suffering can contribute to development, maturity, and fulfillment. It is through adversity that many times an inner attitude is developed which allows one to triumph over tremendous personal anguish. It can be in the encounter with bereavement, loss, and deprivation that creative response is released. Courage is found to face seemingly insurmountable odds, and self-growth is the result. Tournier reminds us that "the lives of sufferers demand permanent courage, a constant expenditure of courage; and since courage belongs in the spiritual economy, the more one spends it, the more one has. It is like a current flowing through them and producing joy, the joy of victory over one's fate."

So it was with Joseph. Contrary to popular opinion, he did not start with an ideal foundation. Instead, his foundation was extremely weak in many ways. Yet despite less than ideal circumstances, Joseph grew to be one of two major biblical Old Testament characters of which not one negative word is stated (the other being Daniel).

Let's take a look at the dilemmas Joseph had to overcome.

A Less Than Perfect Father

In early life, Jacob, Joseph's father, had been an A#1 turkey. For him the end always justified the means. He was not unlike J.R. Ewing, the character we love to hate from the television series "Dallas." During one episode J.R. was asked by one of the victims of his treacherous schemes how he could live with himself. He gave his famous smirk and with a chuckle answered, "Aw shoot, honey, once you've lost your conscience, the rest is easy." The same could have been said of Jacob in his early life.

Scene One: In Genesis 25 Jacob's brother, Esau, had been out hunting. Famished, he came home from a long day in the wilderness. His nostrils caught the scent of fresh stew being made by his younger brother. Hungry and fighting fatigue, Esau asked Jacob for a hot meal.

Jacob saw his golden opportunity. He would be glad to give Esau some of the stew—for a price. The price was that Esau hand over the birthright. This would make Jacob the rightful heir. He would be thrust into the position of prominence he had envied for so long.

Esau hardly hesitated.

Scene Two: On his deathbed, Isaac (Esau and Jacob's father) was making plans to give Esau the patriarchal blessing. Rebekah, Isaac's wife, overheard his plan and summoned her favorite son, Jacob. Together they devised a plan. While Esau was out hunting, Jacob would put animal skin on his arms. He would then take some venison stew to his father and claim to be Esau. Blind Isaac might feel his arms to make sure it was Esau bringing the stew.

The blessing was given; once again Jacob had come out on top.

Scene Three: Desiring to cover the conspiracy and at the same time save her youngest son from Esau's wrath, Rebekah sent Jacob to her brother, Laban.

Working for his uncle, he fell in love with his cousin Rachel. Laban agreed to a marriage if Jacob would work for him for seven years. Finally the wedding day arrived. At the wedding feast, Jacob no doubt imbibed freely. It wasn't until the following morning that he discovered he had slept not with Rachel, but with her older sister, Leah. Uncle Laban had tricked him.

To get Rachel, Jacob had to work seven more years.

Scene Four: Leah gave Jacob four sons—Reuben, Simeon, Levi, and Judah, but the Bible says tersely, "Rachel was barren" (Genesis 29:31). In order to try to make her contribution, Rachel insisted that Jacob sleep with her handmaidens who would be surrogate mothers for her children. The two servants, Bilhah and Zilpah, produced two sons each—Dan, Naphtali, Gad, and Asher. Not to be outdone, Leah produced three more children, two sons and a daughter: Issachar, Zebulun, and Dinah.

Finally Rachel became pregnant and gave birth. The child, the twelfth in the family, was named Joseph. As a small child, Joseph heard the bickering and felt the anger. Leah and Rachel were at each other's throats. Jealousy haunted the household.

It was not a happy home.

Scene Five: Several years later, in giving birth to her second son, Benjamin, Rachel died. In his mourning, the patriarch Jacob showered his affection on Joseph, Rachel's firstborn. Scripture tells us that Jacob ". . . loved Joseph more than any of his other sons . . ." (Genesis 37:3). Joseph became the apple of his father's eye.

In no way did Jacob try to hide his partiality. He made Joseph a special coat. You may have heard it referred to as the "coat of many colors," but the actual Hebrew word describes it as a robe extending to the ankles and wrists, perhaps with an embroidered narrow stripe of color around the edge. It was a garment worn by nobility and the wealthy. Joseph's brothers wore garments that were short and sleeveless. With such garments, they were able to clamber up hills, wade through swampy areas, and carry sheep on their shoulders.

In essence, Joseph's robe declared that he was exempt from manual labor and hardship. Even the light color of his robe indicated that he did not expect to get dirty or have it soiled in any way from hard work. No wonder his brothers despised him.

But more than that, the garment worn by Joseph commonly marked the rightful heir in the family. Most probably this was the case with Joseph as well. Middle East custom declared that when the oldest son lost the birthright, it then went to the oldest son of the second wife. Reuben, the oldest son, had a sexual affair with his father's concubine. As a result, he had lost the inheritance of the family. Thus, the birthright had fallen at the feet of Joseph.

Shackled by His Siblings

TV "soaps" have nothing on the story of Jacob and his family. I have already mentioned Reuben. Then there was Dinah, who was raped by the son of the town mayor. And then there were Simeon and Levi who, along with their brothers, plotted revenge for Dinah, deceived the young men of the community, and slaughtered them all.

Perhaps the saddest statement in the entire narrative is Jacob's reaction to the sin of his sons. There was no disciplinary action taken that is evidenced. Instead, Jacob's reaction centered upon himself. Concern for his own reputation was preeminent. Scripture records, "Then Jacob said to Simeon and Levi, 'You have brought trouble on me by making me a stench to the Canaanites and Perizzites, the people living in this land . . .' " (Genesis 34:30). It is obvious that there was a total lack of behavioral parameters set by Jacob, the father. Discipline was nowhere to be seen. Joseph's siblings had escaped without punishment once more.

And if you haven't had your fill of sordidness yet, then there was Judah, who, thinking he was sneaking out to have sex with a prostitute, found that he had been sleeping with his daughter-in-law.

That was the "happy little family" in which Joseph grew up. Not only did he have weak, ineffective parents, but he was surrounded with jealous and vicious brothers. It may sound like an ideal TV-soap-opera scenario, but it's not the best kind of setting in which to be raised. And that's where God placed Joseph.

Overcoming the Odds

Assuming that Joseph was a normal adolescent, he probably didn't understand what was happening in his life. The mere negotiation of the obstacle course called adolescence is an awesome feat. To be able to understand it all requires genius.

Without the aid of modern psychology, television, SAT scores, or even a written Bible, Joseph did quite well, thank you! Though we don't know too much about the first seventeen years of Joseph's life, we can still observe several "overcoming" characteristics. As you read through them, you will see how they crop up in his life, but I would also suggest that you check to see if they are present in your life.

Positive mental attitude. Despite the fact that his brothers berated him and were vicious in their jealousy, Joseph looked at life positively. God had something special in store for his life, regardless of his background. He attempted to translate that belief to his brothers through sharing his two dreams. But as Joseph's jealous brothers viewed him, they interpreted his positive attitude as arrogance.

What the brothers didn't understand, and what Joseph did understand, was that your attitude determines your outcome. In fact, often your attitude determines your altitude. Perhaps the following diagram will help:

PERSPECTIVE OF LIFE →
PERCEPTION OF CIRCUMSTANCES →
PERFORMANCE IN LIVING

You can look at life through various perspectives. Your perspective may be influenced by circumstances, environment, and temperament, but the most important ingredient is your will or volition. You determine how you are going to view life, just as Joseph did. Look through the lens of positive realism and there is no limit to what life can hold. On the other hand, look through the inverted lenses of discouragement, disillusionment, and doubt, and life becomes shaded. Nothing goes right and even the positives become negatives. That is why Scripture says, "Finally, brothers, whatever is true, whatever is noble, whatever is right, whatever is pure, whatever is lovely, whatever is admirable—if anything is excellent or praiseworthy—think about such things" (Philippians 4:8).

One of my favorite stories concerns two hunting friends. One of them always saw things from a positive perspective while the other never saw anything positive. One day, the positive sportsman decided he would change his friend.

With this goal in mind, he purchased the finest hunting dog he could find. As duck season was approaching, he taught his dog to retrieve ducks. His method was a little different, however. Rather than teaching the dog to jump into the water and swim to the duck, he taught the dog to walk on water. With great pains and patience, the dog learned quickly.

When duck season arrived, he picked up his colleague and headed for the lake. Having situated themselves in the blind, they began to call for the waterfowl. Before long, a group flew in low. The hunters opened fire, and the ducks began to fall from the sky. The time had come.

With a sharp whistle from the hunter, his dog jumped into the water. As though miraculous, he walked across the water, picked up the ducks, and brought them back to the blind. With pride and amusement on his face, the joyful hunter looked at his friend and queried, "How do you like that?"

"Huh," his fellow hunter replied, "you got stuck with a dog that can't swim, I see."

The one who overcomes the odds in life will always have an attitude that looks up rather than down. His motto may as well be, "Keep your chin up and your knees down."

Perseverance and determination. Although Joseph had numerous weak points in his family foundation, he determined to persevere. He had caught the essence of what Paul would say centuries later: "Do you not know that in a race all the runners run, but only one gets the prize? Run in such a way as to get the prize" (1 Corinthians 9:24). *Run to win!*

Many today simply jog through life. Others have slowed to a walk. Still others are sitting on the sidelines just watching the race. Yet the only way to run the race of life is to run to win. You must always remember that the race of life is not a short sprint that is over quickly. Life is a long-distance endurance run. It requires pacing and, most of all, persistence and determination.

Recently I watched the video highlights of the 1984 summer Olympics. Jeff Blatnick competed in Greco-Roman wrestling, an event in which the United States had never won a medal. Added to the drama was the fact that Jeff had undergone major surgery for cancer only two years before.

As I watched the video, I relived those moments. Blatnick was not to be denied. He was the essence of determination. As the seconds wound down, Blatnick seemed destined to be the gold medal winner. When the final buzzer sounded, the arena erupted.

Camera crews and newscasters rushed in for an interview of the new hero. With tears running down his face, he tried to respond to their questions. The words caught in a knot in his throat—he broke down and cried like a baby. As I sat there watching, mesmerized, I realized there was a lump in my throat and tears were streaming down my cheeks as well. Jeff Blatnick was indeed an overcomer!

This is the attitude that Joseph modeled in his life. Determined never to use excuses to pacify life's challenges, he ran the race to win.

Attitude of service. Today, *serving* seems negative. Most see it as a weakness rather than a strength. Serving is for wimps and losers. But Joseph realized that one of the greatest strengths in life is to give your life away to others. Despite the abuse from his brothers, he still was willing to be of service to them. At his father's request he traveled to where they were working in order to find what their needs were and what he could do to help. How easy it would have been for him to turn away from any act of service to his brothers!

Though the New Testament would be written much later, Joseph understood some of its vital principles. Paul wrote to the Galatians and said, ". . . serve one another in love" (Galatians 5:13). Like Joseph, Jesus served others regardless of their actions toward Him. He said, "For even the Son of Man did not come to be served, but to serve . . ." (Mark 10:45). Later He pointed out that the route to greatness lies in this fact: ". . . whoever wants to become great among you must be your servant" (Matthew 20:26).

I am sure you remember the story of *The Little Engine That Could.* A trainload of toys needed to be delivered to the village for the children. The powerful engine that pulled the passenger trains was asked to help. "I'm too busy pulling important people," was his haughty reply. Next the working engine that pulled long freight trains was approached. "I'm too busy pulling the machinery that runs the world," he retorted.

When all else failed, the little switch engine in the train yard was asked. He knew he was small and did not have great strength, but he was willing to try. Remember what happened as he approached the big hill? All the way up he kept saying, "I think I can! I think I can! I think I can!" Finally reaching the top and cresting the hill, the train edged toward the downward slope. Picking up speed, it raced down the hill and pulled into the village train station with the children cheering its arrival.

That story speaks volumes of a willingness to serve. Even when we are not sure we can handle the task, we ought to be willing to try. Joseph was an overcomer because he was more concerned with giving his life away to others.

Attitude of spontaneous obedience. Though things were not ideal at home, Joseph was spontaneously obedient. In Genesis 37 when his father asked him to go check on his brothers, he didn't even hesitate. Immediately he responded unquestioningly.

This attitude would be reflected throughout Joseph's life not only to his family but to his God. When God indicated a direction Joseph was to take, Joseph followed it with diligence.

The German theologian and martyr Dietrich Bonhoeffer poignantly stated the importance of obedience. "Only he who believes is obedient, and only he who is obedient believes."[1]

In the New Testament Jesus would say that obedience is the prime conduit through which a fresh awareness of God comes. Jesus Himself said, "Whoever has my commands and obeys them, he is the one who loves me. He who loves me will be loved by my Father, and I too will love him and show myself to him" (John 14:21). Even the closing illustration of Jesus' Sermon on the Mount dealt with obedience. He drew an analogy between the man who is obedient and the man who builds his house on a very solid foundation. When the rains of adversity fall and the streams of disillusionment and discouragement arise and the prevailing winds of pain and difficulty blow, the house stands firm. Jesus says our lives will do the same if we are obedient to His Word.

29

The story is told of a young preacher who was being interviewed by a church as the potential senior pastor. The pastor search committee heard him preach in his own congregation and was spellbound by his oratorical abilities. They unanimously voted to ask him to come and preach a trial sermon at their church.

On the Sunday the trial sermon was preached, the young pastor delivered another oratorical gem. The committee was a bit nervous when they realized that he was preaching the same message they had heard him preach in his own church. Despite the fact, nothing was said and the church unanimously voted to call him as the new pastor.

Three months later he arrived for his first Sunday in the new field. When the time for the message arrived, he began to wax eloquent. Fifteen minutes into the sermon many of the people realized that he was preaching the same sermon he had preached during his trial sermon. They shrugged it off as due to nervousness and the newness of the situation.

That night the evening service began. The music was outstanding. The congregation was in high spirits. Then the young pastor began his message. Within five minutes the entire congregation realized it was the same message again. The quickest deacons' meeting in the history of the church was called following the service.

In addressing the young pastor, the deacons said, "Pastor, we believe that you are tremendously gifted. We also believe that you are God's man for our church at this time and we want to affirm you and support you in everything you do. However, we do have one question. Don't you have more than one sermon?" With a slight smile and a twinkle in his eye, the young man replied, "Yes. And when you start living what I'm preaching in the first one, I'll go to my second one."

Somehow, innately, Joseph understood the importance of spontaneous obedience. It will always be the mark of one who has respect for authority. Joseph modeled well the relationship of belief and obedience.

As you have read these characteristics present in Joseph's life, how has yours measured up? How is your A.Q.—your Attitude Quotient? It's very important for, you see, your attitude will determine your altitude, and thus whether or not you will be an overcomer of a weak foundation. Remember: A cracked foundation can be filled with the mortar of godly attitudes.

POINTS TO PONDER

OVERCOMING A WEAK FOUNDATION

1. In your own words state the main emphasis of this chapter.
2. What type of "weak foundations" are experienced by people in our society?
3. Recount in your mind the family history of Joseph.
4. How can difficulties positively contribute to the development of one's character?
5. What impact does "perspective" have in your daily life? How do you establish your perspective? Would you say your perspective is more negative than positive, or more positive than negative? Why?
6. What have you done in the last week to serve someone without expecting something in return?

2

When the Cards Are Stacked Against You

MAXIM:

The abrasive character of others can be the very crucible God uses to purify our own character.

If Life Is a Bowl of Cherries, What Am I Doing in the Pits? Erma Bombeck's all-too-truthful book made us stop and laugh at ourselves. We saw ourselves on every page and were able to laugh our way through our dilemmas. I'm not sure that even Erma could have made Joseph laugh, however. "The pits" for him became more than just a figure of speech.

Like most people desiring to succeed, Joseph had a sense of destiny. He believed that he was out to accomplish great things. But as we saw in our last chapter, it seems as though he was beginning life with the cards stacked against him. Home was anything but peaceful. Today his brothers would probably be diagnosed as hyperactive. His sister was trapped in an unwanted pregnancy. His dad felt that the children ought to be able to "express themselves freely." And perhaps his father's naiveté and favoritism had been the fatal blow to Joseph's relations with his siblings.

Despite these barriers his sense of destiny remained. Genesis 37:5–11 recounts Joseph's dreams for the future. He could not only say, "I had a dream," but, "I had two dreams!" Naturally Joseph felt he had to tell his brothers about them. Perhaps this was because he was naive. Perhaps just the age of seventeen is reason enough. Maybe it was just a lack of experience and wisdom. Whatever the cause, it should not surprise us, having watched families, that Joseph was quick to tell of his vision for the future.

He described to his brothers that the dream included all of them "binding sheaves of grain out in the field." Suddenly his sheaf rose and stood above the rest. The indication seemed to be that his brothers would bow down before him.

Their response tells everything: "Do you intend to reign over us? Will you actually rule us? . . ." (Genesis 37:8.) Containing their anger became a Herculean task. They could read the writing on the wall—and they preferred to see another wall. There Joseph stood in his dignified robe, telling them that one day he was going to be the head honcho. Their verbal response was one of total incredulity. The verbal was backed up by an emotional reaction: ". . . And they hated him all the more because of his dream and what he had said" (v. 8).

Not content, Joseph had to twist the knife by proceeding to tell them of a second dream. In this the sun and moon and eleven stars bowed down to Joseph (Genesis 37:9). If he had left any doubt in reporting the first dream, his message was clear in the second. The stars referred to the brothers. The temperature began to rise dramatically—the brothers were getting hotter by the moment.

Meanwhile Joseph was being stretched in a schizophrenic dilemma. On the one hand his father was showing him extreme favoritism. This seemed to encourage and support the dreams he was having of his seemingly promising future. On the other side, his brothers were collectively beginning to hope for his demise. Undoubtedly he struggled for a sense of balance. We all do that when we wrestle with opposing influences. Perhaps he shared both dreams with his brothers just to try to gain their acceptance and encouragement of what was to be his divinely appointed future. Unfortunately, relationships rarely work like that.

For days, and possibly months, the brothers fumed over the "preposterous" dreams which Joseph had shared with them. Over their dead bodies would he become their superior! One way or the other they would find a way to stop him. Their time finally came when Jacob sent Joseph to see how his brothers were doing as they tended sheep. The Scripture tells of their reaction upon seeing him coming: "Here comes that dreamer! Come now, let's kill him and throw him into one of these cisterns and say that a ferocious animal devoured him. Then we'll see what comes of his dreams" (Genesis 37:19, 20). The die was cast.

But Reuben, the oldest brother, had more maturity and sense. Murder would never work. Instead he set forth the idea of throwing Joseph in the cistern. To cover up their deed, they would strip off his robe and blot it with animal blood. They would then proclaim to their father that their youngest brother had been killed. What an excellent cover-up—just enough to soothe their consciences and ease their guilt.

Precipitation of Adverse Circumstances

It would be helpful to understand the causes that put Joseph "in the pits." They are often the same causes that put us there. These factors are especially evident when others are involved in our being in the pits.

I read regularly in the newspaper of families that have been torn apart by underlying currents of uncontrolled emotion. Often these families stand face-to-face with tragedy. A recent television movie depicted a son and daughter who killed their father because of his anger toward them and mistreatment of them. *The Burning Bed* skyrocketed the career of Farrah Fawcett. Unfortunately, the theme of the movie was not so skyrocketing—a lady sets her husband on fire as he sleeps in bed because of the tragic emotional dilemma within the family.

Emotions can be fuel to the fire in the context of human relationships. They can cause what began as a tiny spark to burst into a raging flame. The heat from the ensuing emotional inferno can severely burn those involved. Let's take a quick look at some of these emotional "matchsticks."

Jealousy. "When his brothers saw that their father loved him more than any of them, they hated him and could not speak a kind word to him" (Genesis 37:4). Webster's Dictionary defines *jealous* as being "intolerant of rivalry ... apprehensive of the loss of another's exclusive devotion; hostile toward a rival or one believed to enjoy an advantage." Joseph's brothers were hostile toward him because of his father's blatant favoritism. Thus jealousy often wreaks havoc based on this premise. Many a home has been tragically destroyed because of this debilitating tendency.

Envy. Having seen the favoritism shown by Jacob to Joseph, the brothers envied the special attention. Why did they not have a special robe like him? Why did they have to work hard when he could just supervise? Why weren't they as handsome? The questions were innumerable. The green-eyed monster had reared its ugly head.

Webster's describes *envy* as one step past jealousy. It is the "painful or resentful awareness of an advantage enjoyed by another joined with a desire to possess the same." They were willing to go to any length to satisfy that envy.

Joseph might have been able to quell some of it. Scripture does not seem to indicate much effort on his part to do so, however. Probably most of the actions on his part were inadvertent. He didn't really mean to strike up envy. But perhaps he didn't stop long enough to take inventory as to what was happening.

Meanwhile, the ravenous appetite of envy was eating at the lives of his brothers. They were sick inside with their desire to be in his shoes. Scripture tells us, "A heart at peace gives life to the body, but envy rots the bones" (Proverbs 14:30).

Bitterness. Because jealousy and envy were allowed to take root in their lives, Joseph's brothers became bitter. Scripture warns us of its deadly effect. Paul tells us, "Get rid of all bitterness, rage and anger . . ." (Ephesians 4:31). The writer of Hebrews warns us again, "See to it that no one misses the grace of God and that no bitter root grows up to cause trouble and defile many" (Hebrews 12:15).

When bitterness takes its stranglehold, excessive amounts of emotional energy are wasted. The present circumstances are never enjoyed to the fullest. Perspective is clouded. Relationships are scarred. Those who hold bitterness become a poisonous influence to all with whom they associate.

Scripture also tells us to ". . . live at peace with everyone" (Romans 12:18). We can only be responsible for taking the initiative on our end of relationships. Another's belligerence is often beyond our control.

So it was that adverse circumstances were precipitated in Joseph's life. Now the question, as he sat in the pit, became how to deal with such circumstances.

Principles for Dealing With Adverse Circumstances

Can you imagine being in Joseph's place? He was in the middle of nowhere and had no help. Was his life going to end here at the ripe old age of seventeen? He had tried crawling up the sides of the cistern only to find it totally impossible. There was no way out. He was surrounded. And what's worse, no one cared.

Would you have given up? It is in adverse circumstances that we find the temptation to do just that. It not only seems that no one cares, but even God doesn't care. "If He cares, why doesn't He get me out of this mess?" Surely such thoughts flooded Joseph's mind.

But God did care! Acts 7:9 tells us, "Because the patriarchs were jealous of Joseph, they sold him as a slave into Egypt. *But God was with him . . .*" (*italics mine*). You see, it's always too soon to throw in the towel. Real courage is the ability to endure five minutes more. Joseph couldn't afford to give up. It has been said that the measure of a man is found in what it takes to make him quit.

Winston Churchill was such a man. While young, he attended a preparatory school by the name of Harrow. Following his time there, he completed his education and served in the military in both India and Africa. At the age of sixty-five, this five-foot, five-inch-tall giant was elected as prime minister of England.

Toward the end of his career he was invited to address the student body at his alma mater. The day preceding his arrival, the headmaster announced, "I would encourage you to bring pen and paper tomorrow. The prime minister will speak and you will wish to note his comments. He is possibly the greatest orator of all time."

The following day the auditorium was packed and each pen hoisted. After a rather effusive introduction, Mr. Churchill stepped to the podium. Graciously he acknowledged all. Then in his powerfully authoritative voice, he rumbled: "Never give up.

Never give up. Never give up. Never! NEVER!" With that, he sat down.

So it is with Joseph and us. We must never give up. Paul described life in the pits well when he said, "We are hard pressed on every side, *but not crushed*; perplexed, *but not in despair*; persecuted, *but not abandoned*; struck down, *but not destroyed*" (2 Corinthians 4:8, 9; *italics mine*).

In his life, Paul was stoned at Lystra, caused riots in Ephesus, was plotted against in Corinth, tossed about in a storm-battered ship, shipwrecked at Malta, and imprisoned numerous times. And these were only a few of his trials! All that happened and yet he could say he was "not crushed . . . not in despair . . . not abandoned . . . and not destroyed."

Paul goes on to teach us in Philippians 3:13, 14 that we should be "forgetting what is behind and straining toward what is ahead . . . press on toward the goal to win the prize for which God has called me [us] heavenward in Christ Jesus" (*brackets mine*). Paul knew well what he spoke of since he most probably wrote from a Roman prison at the end of his life. Yet even here he could not give up. And with such an attitude, he realized that the key was forgetting both the adverse and rewarding circumstances of the past. The goal at that point was to press toward the future and to make his life count where it was. In the same manner Joseph, in order to make a meaningful contribution with his life, would have to forget the adverse circumstances and put them behind him. Further, he could not dwell on the favoritism shown by his father. The jealousy, envy, and bitterness shown by his brothers would have to be forgiven.

And so it is with us. Just to "keep on keeping on" is not enough. We must do so with the right attitude. Our pressing on must be with the goal of recovering from the adversities. We must not abandon the desire to make a meaningful contribution in the lives of those around us. It is never too late to get a fresh start!

Promise in the Midst of Adverse Circumstances

Situations are not always as they seem on the surface. Had Joseph looked around the walls of the pit and taken things at face value, he would have determined his life was over. The God in whom he had trusted would have seemed untrustworthy. The dream of the future would have turned to a living nightmare.

But God tells us in His Word not to look merely on outward circumstances. Nor are we merely to evaluate things from our perspective. God tells us to "trust in the Lord with all your heart and lean not on your own understanding; in all your ways acknowledge him, and he will make your paths straight" (Proverbs 3:5, 6). Notice He doesn't tell us not to use our understanding. Instead, He tells us not to trust totally in our own thought processes. This is due to the fact that our understanding is usually from a limited perspective—our own. Behind seemingly outward circumstances, He may well be at work making the path of our lives travel in the direction He desires.

And even in the pits of life, "... God has said, 'Never will I leave you; never will I forsake you.' So we say with confidence, 'The Lord is my helper; I will not be afraid. What can man do to me?' " (Hebrews 13:5, 6). When things look bleak, God, as promised, will always be there in the midst of them with us. When others seem to abandon us, God remains. When through jealousy, envy, or bitterness, others have pushed us into a pit, God goes right on loving.

It is in the midst of these circumstances that God is working out His plan. Romans 8:28 describes that plan: "We know that in all things God works for the good of those who love him, who have been called according to his purpose." Should we wonder, He elaborates that purpose in verse 29 when He says we are "... to be conformed to the likeness of his Son...."

Notice God does not say that everything that happens to us is necessarily good. Instead He says that "in all things God works for the good." So often in the battle of life we wish this were not the master game plan. We desire and pray for victory and mastery, all the while wishing to avoid the very processes that take us there. We must have our mentality redirected. Through all of our life's experiences, God is working to broaden our capacities and abilities. Characteristics are being fine-tuned. God is taking us through a spiritual expansion program in order to enlarge us to enjoy greater spiritual growth and manifold blessings.

The process does not happen overnight. Just as in growing a crop, "First the blade, then the ear, and after that, the full corn in the ear." It is a timely process in which shortcuts are devastating. As author Miles Stanford stated, "A meteor is on a shortcut as it proceeds to burn out, but not a star, with its steady light so often depended upon by navigators." If we are to possess lasting qualities spiritually, we must allow the time in which they may be produced.

Nor are all the things that occur in one's life necessarily pleasant and wonderful. What is best for us is not always easiest. Several years ago I was out waterskiing with a large group of young people. While slalom skiing, the tip of the ski caught a wake and turned me into a human cartwheel. Upon surfacing and feeling a strange sensation in my left leg, I found that my foot was pointed 180 degrees in the opposite direction. Twisting it around to its correct position, I told no one of the injury. After all, we were there to have a good time.

Five days later when I could no longer stand the pain, I went to the hospital emergency room. An orthopedic surgeon was immediately called and, upon completing X rays, found that I had torn major ligaments and cartilage in the leg. To this day I recall the excruciatingly painful work that was done on the knee. This was followed by four months in a cast from my hip to my ankle. Then came the real affliction—weeks of nerve-shattering exercises to strengthen the leg back to its normal health. Though the medical treatment was best for me in the long run, it was extremely painful at the time. So it is with life.

We do not have to travel through many years as Christians to be able to look back on things that seemed disastrous at the time but which have turned out to work for our good. Disappointments have turned into blessings. In the midst of struggles, there seems to have been a guiding hand that directed us through the maze of life. In all of it, God hammers out the characteristics He desires in our life on the anvil of experience and trial.

So be assured that even from the pit God hears your cry. "The righteous cry out, and the Lord hears them; he delivers them from all their troubles" (Psalms 34:17).

Purpose in Adverse Circumstances

Could it have been that God had a purpose for Joseph's pit? Are there reasons for the pits you have experienced in your life? God uses these dilemmas to begin to work out His divine purpose in our lives. He is forming the tapestry of life which in the end will look beautiful on the surface though underneath there are many knots and hanging strings. Remember, it is the knots and hanging strings that make the tapestry's quality.

God was hammering out the metal in the life of Joseph that He knew was needed. Later we find Him doing the same thing with Israel. In Deuteronomy 8:2 God reveals the purpose of the forty years in the pits which they experienced: "Remember how the Lord your God led you all the way in the desert these forty years, [1] to humble you and [2] to test you in order to know what was in your heart, whether or not you would keep his commands" (*brackets mine*).

God is in the process of showing us our inability to handle life without dependence upon Him. Humility comes in realizing that we are not as self-sufficient as we think we are. Often God can only get our attention when we find ourselves in the midst of trials and have reached the end of our rope. It is as we hang there that we are in a position where we can truly hear His voice.

Unfortunately, even there, too often we are looking for an easy way out or still attempting to accomplish our own self-centered purposes. A story is told of a young man walking along a mountain path watching the sun set. Captivated by the splendor of color on the horizon, he slipped over the edge and tumbled over the sheer precipice.

The drop was a thousand feet to the canyon floor. Five hundred feet down the sheer face of the cliff, the young man caught himself on a jutting limb. Hanging desperately in midair, he yelled out into the vast expanse of space, "Is anybody out there?"

Remarkably, a deep, resonant voice responded, "Yes, my son, I am here."

The young man yelled back, "Get me out of here!"

Again, the resonant voice came: "Do you totally trust me?"

Getting impatient, the young man yelled, "Of course, I trust you. Get me out of here!"

"If you trust me, LET GO."

Suspended in time and space, the young man hung there momentarily, then shouted, "Is anybody else out there?"

So it is with us. God allows us to be tested to bring us to an end of ourselves. He then tests us to see what is really in our hearts and too often finds out the truth. Could it be that in the midst of some circumstances you are presently experiencing you are trying to hold on to something while God is telling you to let go? Perhaps this is a time of learning what is actually in your heart and not just in your mouth.

James tells us later in Scripture that testing circumstances plus perseverance lead to a mature faith. Mature faith that results in such experiences is complete and lacks nothing for successful living (James 1:3, 4). The word used for *perseverance* is not one which simply means "grinning and bearing the tough circumstances."

Instead it means the ability to turn difficult situations into greatness and glory. It is the ability to see through the surface of difficult situations and to realize that God's hand is in the midst of them working out things for our best. William Barclay calls it "unswerving constancy." So it is in the midst of struggles that real strength comes.

A Challenge From History

August 22, 1741, was a sweltering day in the city of London. An elderly stooped-shouldered man wandered through the streets. His nightly aimless wandering through the streets of the city had become a familiar ritual. His angry mind raced back to the memories of great adulation and then looked to a future of seemingly hopeless despair.

For forty years the bachelor had written operatic music which was the rave of the royalty in both England and the entire continent. Honors had fallen at his feet. He was in demand everywhere.

Then things changed quickly and drastically. Fellow musicians became jealous and bitter. Members of the royal court reacted strongly to his abrasive manner. A rival gained great success, and envy began to grow.

As though that were not enough, a cerebral hemorrhage paralyzed his right side. He could no longer write. Doctors gave little hope for recovery.

The old composer traveled to France and began to soak in baths rumored to have miraculous powers. Doctors warned him about staying in the scalding water for such long periods of time but he ignored their advice. At one point, he stayed in for nine hours at a time. Gradually his weakened muscles began to receive new life. As his health improved, he once again began to write. Soon, to his amazement, his works were being received with rapturous applause. Honors again began to flow. Life seemed to be heading for the stars. But then he found himself in the pits once more.

Queen Caroline, who had been his staunch supporter, died. England found itself on hard economic times. Wasting heat to warm a theater was viewed as ridiculous. His shows were canceled. And now he found himself wandering aimlessly through the streets once again.

Having wondered where in the world God was, he wandered back home. Opening his door, he found a wealthy gentleman waiting in his living room. The man was Charles Gibbon, who had startled England by rewriting Shakespeare.

Gibbon explained that he had just finished writing a text for a musical that covered the entire Old and New Testament. He believed that the gifted musician was the man to set it to music. He gave the manuscript to the composer and challenged him to write. As he walked out the door, Gibbon turned long enough to say, "The Lord gave me those words."

The great maestro scoffed at the audacity of the young man. No one had ever challenged George Frederick Handel to write something he had not thought of first. Handel's temper was violent and he was a dominating presence among his enemies. Why had Gibbon not brought an opera that was more the composer's cup of tea?

Indifferently he began to read. Suddenly portions of the passage leaped from the page. His eyes fell on such words as "He was despised, rejected of men . . . he looked for someone to have pity on him, but there was no man; neither found he any to comfort him." His eyes raced ahead to "He trusted in God . . . God did not leave his soul in hell . . . He will give you rest." And finally the words stopped at "I know that my Redeemer liveth . . . rejoice . . . hallelujah."

He picked up his pen and began to write. Music seemed to flow through his mind as though it had been penned up for years. Putting music to the script, he finished the first part in seven days. The second section was completed in nine more. Part three was completed in six days and two days were given to fine-tuning the instrumentation. Thus, at the age of fifty-seven, Handel completed the *Messiah* in a mere twenty-four days.

Many know that when the classical work was first performed in London and the "Hallelujah Chorus" was reached, King George II stood because he was so greatly moved. To this day people still rise to their feet as a sign of worship of God and admiration of this great work of art.

Handel, like Joseph, had to deal with the pits of life. But the strength to do so came from knowing the One who can overcome all of the pits. How about you? Do you know the God who is able to rescue you from the cisterns of life? Do you see His hand even in the pit in which you may find yourself? Perhaps the pit is merely a brief stopping place on the road to greatness.

POINTS TO PONDER

WHEN THE CARDS ARE STACKED AGAINST YOU

1. Explain in your own words what it means to have a "sense of destiny." Do you have one?

2. Do you feel Joseph was a bit tactless with his brothers? How do most people respond to such circumstances?

3. What were the main points of tension in Joseph's family? Who was responsible?

4. Recall the difference between *jealousy, envy,* and *bitterness.* How do they relate to each other? Could it be that you are struggling with any of these in your present situation?

5. How does God use adverse circumstances in our lives? What promises has He made to us in the midst of these difficult times?

6. Could you identify with the story of the young man who fell off the cliff and yelled, "Is anybody else out there?" When and why have you felt like crying those same words?

3

The Devil Made Me Do It

MAXIM:

Temptations may cause us to stumble, but we determine whether we fall.

While driving home from work recently, I was mentally reviewing the day's events. The temperature was a balmy seventy-five degrees. Trees rustled with a gentle breeze. The sky was a beautiful Carolina blue. The day had been a profitable one.

Suddenly my reverie was shattered. A fellow motorist rudely cut in front of me, almost forcing me into an oncoming car. Frantically I fought for control. After what seemed an eternity, I regained my position in traffic and my palpitations subsided.

It was only then that I noticed his bumper sticker. It read: IF IT FEELS GOOD, DO IT. From somewhere there came a definite urge to mash the pedal to the metal and turn our automobile ride into a thrilling game of bumper cars. There was a desire in me to be driving an old clunker with 15,000 pounds of "demolition derby power." I could envision my teaching this smart aleck a lesson.

My fantasy continued. He would jump out of the car screaming about my object lesson. Calmly I saw myself getting out of the car saying, "But I was just doing what you told me to do." When he demanded an explanation, I would respond, "You told me that if it feels good I should do it, and it felt great!"

Temptation had struck again. It is an insidious little devil. Coming at the most unexpected moments, it springs from the least likely direction.

Oh well, I had nothing to worry about. After all, "the devil made me do it."

That line was made famous by Flip Wilson and his buxom alter ego named Geraldine. We liked the ring of it so much that we all picked it up immediately. The devil started getting blamed for more things by more people than even he could probably count.

So it was with Joseph. Though the cards had been stacked against him, he had survived the vicious treachery of his brothers. He now found himself in Egypt. And considering, things hadn't turned out too badly. He was the servant of the captain of the guard for Pharaoh. If you had to be a slave for someone, this was better than most.

Things became even better.

The Lord was with Joseph and he prospered, and he lived in the house of his Egyptian master. When his master saw that the Lord was with him and that the Lord gave him success in everything he did, Joseph found favor in his eyes and became his attendant. Potiphar put him in charge of his household, and he entrusted to his care everything he owned.

From the time he put him in charge of his household and of all that he owned, the Lord blessed the household of the Egyptian because of Joseph. The blessing of the Lord was on everything Potiphar had, both in the house and in the field. So he left in Joseph's care everything he had; with Joseph in charge, he did not concern himself with anything except the food he ate.

Genesis 39:2–6

Things were definitely on their way up! What had been such a tragic beginning could turn into a triumph. Perhaps there was a silver lining in every cloud.

Then it happened. Temptation sprang from nowhere. Potiphar's wife had been eyeing Joseph and had determined he was a real "hunk." Besides that, life was getting a bit boring and everybody ought to have an affair at least once.

The first day she propositioned him, he was probably startled. He had just been striving to do his best and earn the respect of his boss. Now his boss's wife was putting the move on him. Perhaps for a moment he wondered what he should do. Where would he go? If he surrendered to her, maybe she could be of benefit to him, get him a raise in salary. Besides, it might be enjoyable. Whoever said that sin wasn't fun, didn't know what they were talking about.

Then his more sane thoughts quickly returned. "With me in charge, my master does not concern himself with anything in the house; everything he owns he has entrusted to my care. No one is greater in this house than I am. My master has withheld nothing from me except you, because you are his wife. How then could I do such a wicked thing and sin against God?" (Genesis 39:8, 9).

Joseph's choice involved honor or the boss's wife, but temptation comes in many forms. For Solomon it was polygamy. By giving in, he allowed his wives to lead him astray from the God who had made him king. For David it was lust. In bowing to the temptation, he found himself committing murder to cover his deed. The ramifications affected his family for years. For Moses it was anger. Through his display of impatience, he was not allowed to enter the Promised Land even after forty hard years in the desert. For Judas it was money and recognition. His betrayal of Christ only led to a tragic ending as he took his own life.

Each of us has weak points. One thing we can be sure of is that temptation is inevitable. Even Christ was not exempt. Immediately following His baptism and God's endorsement of His ministry, He was led into the wilderness for testing. Scripture records that the Adversary came to Christ three times in temptation (Matthew 4:1–11). First Christ was tempted to use His own powers and strengths selfishly. He had been fasting forty days and forty nights. Why didn't He turn some of the stones on the ground into bread? After all, they probably resembled the small fragrant loaves cooked in Israelite homes regularly. Memory of the warm fragrance of homemade bread must have played havoc with His mind. But He resisted.

Again, the devil came, tempting Him to see how far God would go in protecting Him. Not only was God's provision tested, the temptation to perform the spectacular was great. After all, everyone is drawn to someone who can perform the amazing. Why not gather a following quickly through such a captivating display?

Again the answer was NO.

Finally the challenge came to compromise. By meeting Him halfway the devil promised Him great rewards. Besides, what's so wrong with a minor hedging of your bets?

One last time a resounding refusal was heard.

Like Joseph and Jesus, we are often tempted the most in the midst of success. Joseph's life was going well. Everything was in order. Jesus, on the other hand, had just launched a successful ministry. What better endorsement than that of God Himself could there possibly be! Yet it was at those very times the greatest temptations came.

So it is with us. At the very heights of life are the possibilities for the greatest falls. Strengths and gifts can as easily be misused as used. And since we only go around once, why not get all the gusto we can out of life? And what's so bad about compromises? Perhaps no one will ever know.

In dealing with temptation it is important to remember where it originated. It started very early in Scripture when in Genesis 3:1 the devil came to Eve and questioned God's directive. Challenging her to do it her way, he paved the way for the greatest disaster in human history. Similarly, he instigated a potential trap for Joseph and Jesus. He does the same for us.

Paul warns us to be "aware of his schemes" (*see* 2 Corinthians 2:11). In 2 Corinthians 11:14 he tells us that "Satan himself masquerades as an angel of light." He is constantly attempting to deceive us to get us off the right track. "Be self-controlled and alert. Your enemy the devil prowls around like a roaring lion looking for someone to devour" (1 Peter 5:8).

This is beginning to sound serious.

But can't we always rely on the fact that "the devil made me do it"? Now for the bad news. No, we cannot rely on that fact. James teaches us that when we give in to temptation, it is not the devil's fault at all. Temptation itself is not sin. If it were, Christ would have been sinful and therefore would not have been the perfect Savior. Instead, temptation is only an opportunity to sin. It is not the devil who makes us do it at all but rather we ourselves. The Scripture says, "Each one is tempted when, by his own evil desire, he is dragged away and enticed. Then, after desire has conceived, it gives birth to sin; and sin, when it is full-grown, gives birth to death" (James 1:14, 15).

God is not to blame. Our fellowmen are not to blame. Not even Satan is to be blamed. The problem is us!

The word in the original for *dragged away* gives the picture of a fish being drawn to bait and not aware of the deadly hook that lies hidden inside. The word translated *enticed* means to be ensnared.

It is the picture of a fish or animal that is caught in a trap and cannot get away. Remember that lust when it is conceived brings sin and sin ends in death. Every time a person gives in to temptation not only a part of him dies but so does a part of our society.

It sounds as though a battle is raging about us, doesn't it? It is! So how are we to deal with it? I believe that Paul best answers our questions in Ephesians 6. There he tells us that life is a struggle. The picture he paints in the original language is a hand-to-hand combat to the death. No simple scrimmage is this, but rather all-out war.

We are told that we are wrestling with the devil and his accomplices. To get the full force of Paul's description we must realize that wrestling in his day was vastly different from the wrestling we see in the Olympics of our day. In Rome the goal was not to pin the opponent's shoulders to the mat but rather to pin his neck. Having done so, if the crowd's pleasure was death, the victor would squeeze the life from his unfortunate opponent. And so Paul warns us to take the Adversary's role seriously. In order to stand firm against temptation's onslaught, we must make sure we are standing in the power that only God can give our lives. The only way to do this is by putting on what the Scripture refers to as "the full armor of God."

This armor is comprised of elements that must be in our lives to make them stable and strong. First Paul tells us to put on the "belt of truth" (Ephesians 6:14). The belt for the soldier in Paul's day held the tunic in place around the waist. It gave him freedom of movement in the midst of battle. It was also a place where medals of valor won in battle were hung. Commanders often awarded their officers belts trimmed with gold, silver, and precious stones as a reward for outstanding heroism.

The belt was the central anchor for the soldier's battle gear. So it is with our lives. Truth, as it is used here, represents honesty, lack of hypocrisy, and sincerity. Perhaps it could best be labeled as integrity. It is the life in which the cracks and defects are not falsely covered over or hidden. Truth is not compromised. Instead there is a sincerity in all that is done.

The Psalmist tells us that there must be "truth in the inner parts . . ." (51:6). The Proverbs proclaim, "Truthful lips endure forever, but a lying tongue lasts only a moment" (12:19). Perhaps Mark Twain, that sage philosopher, was saying the same thing when he said, "When in doubt, tell the truth."

Donald Seibert, former chief executive officer of JCPenney Corporation, wrote of this quality in his book *The Ethical Executive.* Siebert, an outstanding Christian leader, said, "Among the people that I know at the top of the nation's major corporations, the personal quality that is regarded most highly is a solid, unwavering sense of integrity."[1]

We must be aware that truthfulness can be compromised in many ways. An intentional overstatement to build up our own image can crumble our credibility.

In high school I determined to go out for the school baseball team. In pushing hard to make the team, I overextended myself and hurt my right arm. As a result, I was not able to make the cut and discouragement set in. Seeing my frustration, the coach stepped in to help. He wondered if I would be willing to serve as manager of the team. Assuming that something was better than nothing, I took the position.

When the season was over, varsity letters were awarded. To my surprise I found that I had been chosen to receive one as the team manager. The symbol for baseball was two bats crossed with a baseball in between. The symbol on the varsity letter for manager was M.G.R.

Proudly I took my letter to the sport shop. There they were to attach the two emblems to the letter and then the letter to the varsity sweater. When I picked it up a few days later, I noticed they had left off the M.G.R. I quickly determined not to say a thing.

In the weeks and months that followed an interesting thing occurred. When girls would come around and ask if I had been a part of our school's team, I would simply smile and say yes. I found it much more rewarding not to add the fact that I had served as the manager of the team. I was striving to increase my image through intentional oversight. Perhaps a double standard is the ultimate reversal of wearing the "belt of truth." For many it is easy to put on the religious mask, say the religious words, and go through the religious motions on Sunday. Just as easily, the religious exterior is shed on Monday. This is why Jesus said, "Not everyone who says to me, 'Lord, Lord,' will enter the kingdom of heaven, but only he who does the will of my Father who is in heaven" (Matthew 7:21).

Perhaps one of the most difficult truths to deal with is the truth about ourselves. We find it very easy to criticize the other person without seeing the shortcomings in our own life. Christ challenges us, "Why do you look at the speck of sawdust in your brother's eye and pay no attention to the plank in your own eye? How can you say to your brother, 'Let me take the speck out of your eye,' when all the time there is a plank in your own eye? You hypocrite, first take the plank out of your own eye, and then you will see clearly to remove the speck from your brother's eye" (Matthew 7:3–5). One of the keys, then, of a life of truth is facing the truth about ourselves. When there are things lacking in our lives or in need of change, we must be brave enough to step up to them and make the needed alteration.

Second, Paul tells us to put on the ". . . breastplate of righteousness" (Ephesians 6:14). The breastplate in biblical days covered two major areas: the heart and the bowels. In biblical thought the heart most often represented the thoughts. This is seen in Proverbs 23:7 where we are told, "For as he thinketh in his heart, so is he . . ." (KJV). The bowels represented the emotions. Jeremiah 31:20 says, ". . . my bowels are troubled for him . . ." (KJV). Has it really changed? Don't our bowels still represent our emotions? If not, why is there Maalox?

In order to protect these areas the breastplate of righteousness is needed. This comes from a life that has experienced the righteousness of God as a result of being in right relationship with Him. Because of that relationship, righteousness can be practiced in everyday life. Perhaps nowhere in Scripture is a life-style of righteousness better described than in 2 Peter 1:3–8. The qualities listed there are poignant:

Goodness   This refers to excellence and courage in life. As we strive for excellence in all that we do, we are not ashamed to tell others why we do so. We are to excel in our efforts and have the courage to give God the glory.

Knowledge   This means practical wisdom to decide rightly when major decisions must be made. It also carries with it the duty of acting honorably in all situations.

Self-control   This pictures life that is in proper control. Care is taken not to have "hoof and mouth disease" due to misuse of the tongue. The body is to look like the temple of God, not the city dump. Thought life is to be kept on a higher plane. The computer maxim "garbage in, garbage out" is to be heeded when feeding the mind.

Perseverance   This is brave and courageous acceptance of circumstances. It is far removed from the mere gritting of teeth and stoically enduring. It is to see God's creative process in motion in the midst of adversity.

<u>Godliness</u>	This relates to being in a right relationship vertically so that our relationships horizontally can be effective. Ruptured fellowship with God will drastically affect our relationship with our fellowman or vice versa. Both must be in balance.
<u>Love</u>	This is the kind of self-giving that sees people as important. They are not seen as nuisances or interruptions. Rather they are the most important assets in our lives.

Thus it is that our thoughts and emotions are protected. As the righteousness of God has been given to us through His grace, so we live out His righteousness in daily conduct. Thus we will have a clear conscience and settled emotions.

Third, we are told to have our "feet fitted with the readiness that comes from the gospel of peace" (Ephesians 6:15). Most probably here Paul referred to having both peace with God and the peace of God through a right relationship with Him. Though Christ had not come in Joseph's day, in our day this is obtained through a personal relationship with Jesus Christ. It is through acceptance of Him as Lord and Savior that we gain such peace (Romans 5:1, 2). Likewise, on its heels comes the peace of God in all circumstances. Here is found the unwavering peace in the midst of life's storms. Worry is eliminated. Steadiness prevails (*see* Philippians 4:6, 7). So it is with such peace that we are able to keep a strong footing in the midst of life's scrimmages.

Fourth, we are to "take up the shield of faith . . ." (Ephesians 6:16). Here we find total trust in God alone in every situation.

In 1890 Harry Blondin stretched a tightrope across Niagara

Falls. A thousand feet of rope stretched tautly 160 feet above the falls was his walkway. Carefully he traversed the rope only to return to a cheering mass of spectators. He then asked if they believed he could take a specially designed wheelbarrow and push it across the rope. With unanimous exuberance they affirmatively responded. And push it he did.

Upon return to his starting point, he then asked his most challenging question. Who would sit in the wheelbarrow as he pushed it across? One by one the spectators chose to pass. Their trust was complete as long as it cost them nothing. Only when they had to put things on the line did the fickleness of their faith appear.

Sounds familiar, doesn't it? But Paul says if we are to ward off the attacks of the Adversary our lives must be lived by faith. The writer of Hebrews tells us: "Without faith it is impossible to please God . . ." (11:6). We are directed to "live by faith, not by sight" (2 Corinthians 5:7). But it is so much easier to go by sight.

If the battle is to be won, faith must be exhibited.

Fifth, Paul tells us to put on the "helmet of salvation . . ." (Ephesians 6:17). As the helmet protects the head, so it symbolizes assurance. Unless one is certain of his personal relationship with God, he is destined to fall. The Adversary would try to whittle us down with the dual-edged sword of doubt and discouragement. And so we must respond with a strong confidence as in 1 John 5:13, 14: "I write these things to you who believe in the name of the Son of God so that you may know that you have eternal life. This is the assurance we have. . . ."

We must sing with hymn writer R. Kelso Carter:

Standing on the promises that cannot fail,
When the howling storms of doubt and fear assail,
By the living word of God I shall prevail,
Standing on the promises of God.

How easy it is to say. How complicated it is to do.

Last, Paul tells us to take up "... the sword of the Spirit, which is the word of God (Ephesians 6:17). Here Paul speaks not of the huge broad sword wielded with great slashes in battle. Rather, he speaks of the short dagger *machaira* approximately eighteen inches long. It was used in hand-to-hand combat. It was easy to maneuver to both parry an enemy's strike as well as tender a strategic thrust.

As the writer speaks of the "word of God," he is not referring to God's total revealed Word or *logos*. Instead here he refers to the individual Scripture which the Spirit brings to our remembrance in time of need. It is the Word applied (the *rhema*). The prerequisite, of course, is to be familiar with what God's Word says.

Perhaps that is our real problem. We just aren't familiar with what God's Word says. A few years ago I sat at a conference in Dallas, Texas, listening intently to the dynamic speaker who was a strong leader in student ministries. Suddenly in the midst of his message, he stopped and confronted us with some very key questions.

First, he asked, "How many of you here have been Christians for at least five years?" Ninety percent of those across the auditorium raised their hands.

Second, he queried, "How many of you who have been Christians for five years really have a love for the Lord in your life?" Everybody's hand went up.

Third, he questioned, "How many of you who have been Christians for five years and who really have a love for the Lord truly desire to become all He wants you to be?" Again, all hands remained held high.

Then he dropped the hammer. "How many of you who have been Christians for five years, who really love the Lord, who desire to become everything He wants you to be, can stand up right now and quote twenty-five verses of Scripture by memory?" You could have heard a pin drop. Two hands remained in the air out of over sixty people.

Sometime later I was in the state of Washington. I had the opportunity to be in a home where I found myself confronted with the privilege to share Christ with a young woman. As I was walking through the Gospel with her, her little girl entered the room and listened intently. We were talking about what the Bible has to say about Jesus Christ. Suddenly the child jumped in and questioned as she pointed to the family Bible on the table, "Mommy, is that God's Book?" With a smile only a mother can give, she responded, "Yes, dear, it sure is."

Not to be stilled, the daughter piped up, "If it's God's Book, then why don't we give it back to Him, because we sure never use it." I could see the mother turning eighteen shades of red.

But the little girl was saying something that really needed to be said. Perhaps what she said applies to many of us. Our talk far surpasses our walk. When we really get down to the bottom line, we talk about knowing more of God's Word than we actually do.

How about you? Have you put any of God's Word to memory this last year? Could you have answered in the affirmative concerning putting five verses of Scripture to memory for every year you've been a Christian? Can you say with David, "Oh, how I love your law!"

> The law of the Lord is perfect, reviving the soul.
> The statutes of the Lord are trustworthy, making wise the simple.
> The precepts of the Lord are right, giving joy to the heart.
> The commands of the Lord are radiant, giving light to the eyes . . .
> They are more precious than gold, than much pure gold;
> They are sweeter than honey, than honey from the comb.
>
> Psalms 19:7, 8, 10

The Scripture tells us that it is "God-breathed." Second Timothy 3:16 states: "All Scripture is God-breathed and is useful for teaching, rebuking, correcting and training in righteousness." If my life is to be guided by God's word, I must realize that it will help me in four different areas:

Teaching	Showing the direction and manner in which we should be living.
Rebuking	Showing us where we go wrong.
Correcting	Showing us how to get back on the right path when we have veered away.
Training in righteousness	Showing us how to keep on living successfully.

Second Timothy 3:17 completes the purpose of God's Word in our lives: "So that the man of God may be thoroughly equipped for every good work."

Though Paul's words had yet to be written, the characteristics mentioned by Paul are clearly seen in Joseph's life. It was as though they were etched in Joseph's mind. They were then lived out in his daily life. For Joseph there was no conscious "putting on the armor of God" as Paul would picture it later. There was, however, a commitment to the character qualities that make up that armor. His life emanated sincerity and honesty. He did not strive to be something he was not. Nor was he tempted to use his position and power for self-centeredness.

Likewise, practical righteousness characterized his life-style. He strove for excellence in all that he did so that God might be glorified. He sought practical wisdom to be able to handle the strains of daily living. It was that wisdom that enabled him to make the decision not to be lured by Potiphar's wife. He had a mastery of his life that did not allow him to give in to weakness. Doubtless in the midst of temptation, he knew that God was with him. It was his godliness, derived from a proper vertical relationship, that allowed him to handle the horizontal dimension of life—including the pressure of temptation.

To these qualities God has given us a jump on Joseph. Standing on this side of the Old Testament, we are able to see God's provision through the Gospel. We are able to have assurance of a personal relationship with God through His Son, Jesus Christ. No longer do we have to wonder or hope that we are acceptable in God's sight. Now we know we are, based on the authority of God's Word.

Scripture has sketched out for us the meaning of faith. As opposed to Joseph, who merely had a basic understanding, we have been given the opportunity to see faith in full form. God tells us that it is transferring our trust from our own efforts, intellect, or abilities to Him alone. Thus we can be ". . . sure of what we hope for and certain of what we do not see" (Hebrews 11:1).

Most importantly, whereas Joseph only had experience, we now have revelation. God has made Himself known through His Word. All we must do is have ears that are willing to hear and a mind that is willing to believe. With those two ingredients we can know the mind of God as made known through His Scripture. What an edge God has given us over Joseph. Now the key question is, "Will we take advantage of it?"

Joseph handled temptation by resisting. Things haven't changed over these vast number of centuries. The best way even today to handle temptation is to flee from it. That is why Peter tells us that we are to "resist him [the devil], standing firm in the faith . . ." (1 Peter 5:9). As did Joseph, we are bringing our lives into submission with God. Having determined to stand strong against the Adversary and resist him, we are promised that he will flee from us (James 4:7).

Lest you are struggling with a temptation lately that seems more than you can bear, let's close by looking at a few words of encouragement from God. At times temptation seems stronger than you are capable of thwarting. It seems so overpowering. So irresistible! In such situations God does not leave you without words of support. We have been promised, "No temptation has seized you except what is common to man. And God is faithful; he will not let you be tempted beyond what you can bear. But when you are tempted, he will also provide a way out so that you can stand up under it" (1 Corinthians 10:13). For Joseph, and for you, often the way out is to get away from that which is tempting you.

Remember the next time you are tempted that you face an opportunity to fall or to stand firm. While the temptation may pose a test, there is always a way out. Temptation may cause you to stumble but only you will determine whether or not you fall.

POINTS TO PONDER

THE DEVIL MADE ME DO IT

1. In what areas of life was the Lord with Joseph? How was it evidenced in his work? His employer's attitude toward him? What is your boss's attitude toward your work?
2. What is the difference between temptation and sin?
3. What important principles about handling temptation did you learn from the temptation of Christ? What can you do to employ those principles in your life?
4. How did Joseph overcome temptation? Who is responsible when you give in to temptation?
5. Recall Paul's description of the armor of God. What quality was portrayed by:
    The belt of truth
    The breastplate of righteousness
    Feet fitted with the readiness of the Gospel
    The shield of faith
    The helmet of salvation
    The sword of the spirit
    Are these qualities evident in your life? Why or why not?

4
Who, Me?
Handling Unjust
Accusations

MAXIM:

To be falsely accused and retaliate is natural; to be accused and remain in control is supernatural!

Soon after enrolling in kindergarten, I found myself becoming a regular tenant of the "unhappy room" (my creative teacher's version of the corner). A portion of each day seemed to be relegated to this character-building routine. Such varied and sundry activities as kissing girls, putting frogs in the teacher's desk, and pulling fire alarms sent me marching off to my exile.

By the time I reached first grade my reputation had preceded me. Miss Nendle (a female Ichabod Crane) awaited my arrival with a jaundiced eye. And who was I to disappoint her? Each day my mother met me at the door of our home with the teacher's report of my latest dastardly deeds. Unfortunately, all the reports could have been labeled "true and confirmed."

And then it happened. Being the "innocent" soul I was, I still cannot believe it happened. We were at recess. Marilyn was a young lady in our class who was big for her age (she could have started on most high school football teams). Some of the fellows decided to let Marilyn know what they thought of her. In the loving sensitivity of typical first graders they called, "Hey Baby Huey! You can have a job as the Goodyear Blimp when you grow up."

I found myself rolling on the ground in laughter (with great dignity, of course). I could just see her suspended in the clouds. It was then I felt the ground shake. She was thundering toward me. My friends quickly volunteered, while pointing at me, "He said it." Yes, you guessed it. She cleaned my clock! As the fur was flying, I remembered swearing that I would get even with those guys if it was the last thing I did. Unjust accusation had caught me by surprise.

Joseph could have identified with me. Or perhaps more realistically, I could identify with Joseph. Probably so can you.

Just as he seemed destined for higher things, the bottom fell out once again for young Joseph. Having been sold into slavery by his brothers, he finally arrived in Egypt. There he had undoubtedly been auctioned off. His youth, muscled body, and charismatic appeal must have commanded a handsome sum.

His new master, Potiphar, placed him in charge of his entire estate. This man of great clout in Pharaoh's government came to trust Joseph totally. Potiphar could not have been more pleased. Rather than a contemptuous slave, Joseph was a loyal and confident servant and manager. Joseph fulfilled his duties with excellence. His work reflected both effectiveness (getting the right things done) as well as efficiency (getting things done in the right way). As a result, his efforts were rewarded handsomely and God continued to bless him.

Excellence always draws attention. It grabbed the attention of his brothers and they were filled with resentment. Now it drew the attention of his master's wife. For whatever reason she saw Joseph as a conquest and set out to possess him. Sometimes it just seems a guy cannot win for losing!

As we saw in the last chapter, she cunningly set her trap. Her web of seduction became a sticky one. What a series of emotions Joseph must have experienced when the boss's wife propositioned him. Potiphar had entrusted into Joseph's hands everything— everything, that is, except his wife. Realizing the monumental danger, Joseph politely but firmly refused the advances of his supervisor's wife.

It was then that things began to fall apart.

Then one day as he was in the house going about his work—as it happened, no one else was around at the time— she came and grabbed him by the sleeve demanding, "Sleep with me." He tore himself away, but as he did, his jacket slipped off and she was left holding it as he fled from the house. When she saw that she had his jacket, and that he had fled, she began screaming; and when the other men around the place came running in to see what had happened, she was crying hysterically. "My husband had to bring in this Hebrew slave to insult us!" she sobbed. "He tried to rape me, but when I screamed, he ran, and forgot to take his jacket."

She kept the jacket, and when her husband came home that night, she told him her story.

"That Hebrew slave you've had around here tried to rape me, and I was only saved by my screams. He fled, leaving his jacket behind!"

Genesis 39:11–18 TLB

Seemingly life had turned its back once more on Joseph. How was it possible that he could live so right and things still go so wrong? Was life really fair?

If we live a good life, we feel we should be exempt from such things as Joseph experienced. If we do something terrible and receive blame, that is one thing. You could even call that fair. But to live life by the book and be accused unjustly just isn't the way it should be!

Nowhere does Scripture paint this picture, however. Some of God's greatest people have suffered tremendously from unjust situations. The children of Israel unjustly accused Moses of the lack of proper leadership. David was unjustly attacked by Saul when the king saw David as a threat. And what greater illustration is there of unjust accusation than the life of our Lord Himself!

Seduction by your boss's spouse (or even the boss) has most likely not been your encounter with false accusation. Nevertheless, you can most probably identify with the predicament of this scenario. For you the circumstances may be different, but the results just as disastrous.

Perhaps production parts at the job were damaged and someone fingered you to take the fall.

A vital report was lost and since you were the one who typed it, you must be the culprit.

A possible project was mentioned in passing conversation by your boss (though never assigned). Now he wants to know why you have not completed it.

You were given a specific project to see through. The problem was, though given the responsibility for the job, you are not given the needed authority. Now they want your head on a platter.

Perhaps closer to home may be that your seven-year-old has just assaulted you with the accusation, "You are just not fair! All my friends get to do it. You are the meanest parent I have ever seen!"

Regardless of your particulars, why does false accusation occur? We need to understand some of its root causes so that we may be able to deal with its effect. As we will see, several of these causes appeared in Joseph's life.

Unjust accusation can come from an attempt *to cover wrongdoing.* This is dramatically evidenced in Potiphar's wife. Advances had been rejected. Her fantasy affair had not materialized into reality.

In case her flirtatious conduct backfired, she wanted to be covered. The motto "the best defense is a good offense" was being fleshed out in her treacherous dealings. Unfortunately, it was Joseph's flesh at stake.

Have you ever noticed that no one wants to be found in the wrong? We don't have to wait long in life to witness this reality. If our children's rooms look like a tornado just moved through, it is always their "friend" who did the damage. If someone's feelings get trampled as children are playing, it requires a magician to keep up with the quickness of hands as accusing fingers are pointed at each other. If an expensive lamp is knocked over and broken, it is always the younger brother or sister or the dog who is the culprit.

Has someone falsely blamed you to cover their own misdeeds? Have you been left holding an empty bag? Self-preservation can be an incredibly strong motive.

Second, there arises a *desire to punish others for refusing to go along.* Pressure to "go along to get along" can be overpowering. Kids face it every day at school. Executives face it daily in the marketplace. Women fighting for advancement on the job are pounded with it.

When one finds the strength to stand against this type of pressure, it can infuriate those applying the squeeze. A no can be taken as a personal affront by those attempting to put us in a compromising position.

In actuality, those doing the tempting often wish (perhaps subconsciously) that they had the strength to refuse as well. Not having the strength, however, their perception of reality is blurred. Since all detest rejection (perceived or real), they set out on a mission to get even. Again, Joseph found himself caught in this very trap.

Third, there is a strong temptation to *make oneself look better than another.* Being the manipulative creatures we are, we are tempted to do whatever it takes to allow us to come out on top. Recent books have projected this theme with titles such as *Looking Out for Number One* and *Power Through Intimidation.* This is not always accomplished by accusatory statements. It can be done when someone is being falsely blamed and we know the facts, yet remain silent. Open-ended statements can also crucify the character of another. How easy it is to say that a fellow executive left for lunch with his secretary, while not bothering to add that four others went with them. Perhaps the one making the open-ended comment would stand to gain if the executive's ethics and actions were questioned.

The account is told of a first officer of a navy vessel who had a major disagreement with his captain concerning a problem aboard ship. Finally the captain had to pull rank and give a direct command. Disliking the command, the first officer purposely delayed its execution. In response to the disobedience, the captain recorded in the ship's log, "Today the first officer exhibited insubordination."

Vindictively the first officer swore to even the score. Desiring to make the captain look bad while elevating himself he wrote in the ship's log: "Today the captain was sober." What he failed to say was that the captain was sober every day! The pressure to look good can be overpowering.

Fourth, some merely have the *determination to manipulate.* False accusation, or the threat of it, can carry great manipulative power. We see this modeled weekly on such shows as "Dallas," "Dynasty," and "Knots Landing."

Threats can be made to revive old secrets from the past. Weaknesses can be exploited. Strong domineering personalities can find great pleasure in making puppets of weaker constitutions. This is wickedness at its ultimate. And so Potiphar's wife had desired to manipulate Joseph.

It becomes evident that things are not always as they appear at first glance. Perhaps as we gain understanding, at least in part, as to where accusations originate, we can be better equipped to deal with them. Joseph is a perfect model for us. He had cultivated a character which was capable of handling such flagrant attacks.

In the quietness of the early years of his life, Joseph had been occupied with ingraining godly qualities into his character. Many had probably been learned at Rachel's knee. Others came from observing the radical change in his father in response to his life-changing experience with God. These qualities had already aided him when he was in the treacherous hands of his brothers. Now they would have to be called up again as he stood framed by deceit.

Though the written Scripture stood yet in the future, its principles are again evidenced in Joseph's life. Undoubtedly he had heard the stories of Noah and Abraham and how they walked with God. Having seen his father deceitful and self-centered in early life, he must have marveled at the different man that returned from Jabbok. And a God who could make that kind of change in a man was the God upon whom Joseph built his life. That same God undoubtedly etched the maxims of godly living into Joseph's heart. Thus he was equipped to face his new test. Perhaps no section of Scripture better portrays a central guideline of Joseph's life than Psalms 1:1–3, 6.

Blessed is the man who does not walk in the counsel of the wicked or stand in the way of sinners or sit in the seat of mockers.
But his delight is in the law of the Lord, and on his law he meditates day and night.

He is like a tree planted by streams of water, which yields
its fruit in season and whose leaf does not wither.
Whatever he does prospers. . . .
For the Lord watches over the way of the righteous. . . .

Notice the guidelines: First, God's man is careful of his com-
panionship. One who is seeking to be blessed by God must wisely
choose his associates. He is careful to avoid a deadly progression.

Walking with one who does not include God in his plans is dangerous. The "wicked" are not merely those who are grossly evil.
Instead they are people who commit to do everything their way.
God's direction or will might as well not exist. Their theme song
would be "I Did It My Way."

Association can lead to accommodation. However, walking indicates there is at least the possibility to soon part company. The
word used for *wicked* indicates a compulsive determination to live
life according to one's own standards. God is relegated to the shelf
for nothing other than emergency situations.

By this definition the wicked are all around us. It is basically
secular man. He is self-confident—possibly into physical fit-
ness—a mover and shaker. His daily devotional material becomes
the *Wall Street Journal.* It can be your boss, your colleague, your
neighbor next door, or the girl who checks you out at the grocery
counter. Their outlook is based on empirical fact mixed with
existentialism and seems to have little room for faith in a living
God.

Standing indicates a progression from "walking" with the
wicked. The word indicates a lingering in the company of those
who are walking out of step with God. The word used for *sinners*
here is one indicating those living by the wrong values and goals.
To stand with them is to stand with our backs turned from God.
This position becomes harder to change. We face difficulty in re-
moving ourselves from their influence the longer we stand still.

In *sitting* we come to join those who claim religion is for "Holy Joes" and those who need a crutch. They are "mockers." Their rejection of God's principles may be subtle. The Bible is undermined as not truly being God's Word. Church is a great place to be on Sunday but has no relevance for the rest of the week. Even Sunday can be excused if the opportunity comes to play golf, tennis, or leave town. Religion becomes a Christianity of convenience at best.

One writer described the dangerous drifting well when he said, "Beware of first stepping aside from the right path into crooked ways in compliance with evil counsel; secondly, continuing a line of conduct conscience condemns; and last, sitting down at the banquet of sinful pleasure, conscience drugged and scarred, God openly despised."[1]

Joseph realized he could not allow himself to walk, stand, or sit in the presence of those whose lives were not committed to his God. Thus he ran from Potiphar's wife quickly. Likewise, we should not allow ourselves to be drawn aside from the way in which we should be walking.

God's man also makes sure God's directives mark his every step. When he is obedient, God says:

> I will instruct you and teach you in the way you should go; I will counsel you and watch over you.
>
> Psalms 32:8

> He guides the humble in what is right and teaches them his way.
>
> Psalms 25:9

> For this God is our God for ever and ever; he will be our guide even to the end.
>
> Psalms 48:14

73

Whether you turn to the right or to the left, your ears will hear a voice behind you, saying, "This is the way; walk in it."

Isaiah 30:21

Joseph's prayer, like that of the Psalmist in later years, must have been "Teach me your way, O Lord; lead me in a straight path because of my oppressors" (Psalms 27:11). It is the man who is obedient to God's principles that is able to cope with the injustices of life. It is that same man who will see God in a fresh and vital way regularly. Christ said, "Whoever has my commands and obeys them, he is the one who loves me. He who loves me will be loved by my Father, and I too will love him and show myself to him" (John 14:21). Perhaps if God has seemed distant recently, we must stop and realize that it is not He who has moved. It is our obedience that has probably faltered.

Joseph's life was guided by obedience. His walk with God was close even in the midst of adversity. It was for that reason that Joseph was seeing God's hand operative in his daily life.

I recently drove through a marshy area of South Carolina after extremely high winds had ravaged the area. A beautiful, stately tree had been toppled beside the road. Judging by its size, it had stood as a tall sentinel for some time. But this time the wind had come out of its corner with the right one-two combination and the tree was down for the count.

As I looked closer, I discovered a most interesting phenomenon. Though the tree had experienced a good and long life, the root system was amazingly shallow. It had not drilled its way to solid ground. Instead it had remained in the soft, moist, unstable layers of the marsh. As I looked on, I couldn't help but think about how many lives I had seen just like that. They didn't look bad on top but they had no solid root system.

God's Word says that the person who is careful about his companions and whose life is guarded by obedience to God's principles will have a stable and successful life. It will resemble a strong tree firmly rooted. Too often our lives tend to be more akin to trees with shallow root systems. They look marvelous. Unfortunately, when the storms of life come, their anchoring system is inadequate. Over they go.

The life that is rooted in God, on the other hand, has a taproot sunk deep into the God who is bigger than all circumstances. He will be like a palm tree with its taproot deep to weather the storms that would beat it down. It stands erect in spite of the howling wind and driving rain.

So it was with Joseph. In a country where idolatry was the main theology, he carefully guarded his relationship with God. He refused to walk in the counsel of Potiphar's wife. Nor did he stand and linger in the influence of her temptations. He fled from her siren song. His steps were ordered by God's principles. His anchor was strong even in the face of falsehood.

Perhaps we should look at our lives and see how they measure up so far. Are the principles of Psalm 1 governing your life? Are you prepared to handle false accusation as well as Joseph? Or are your roots so shallow that the onslaught of false attack may uproot you?

With some understanding of what was happening in the mind of Potiphar's wife, perhaps Joseph had insight as to the cause behind her false claims. But just how did he react? We have seen the principles that guided his life—the things he did. Now we should pause a moment to look at the things he did not do. These are just as important, as they were a key part in coping with the dilemma.

First, Joseph trusted God completely; therefore, he did not worry. Though the circumstances looked bleak, he looked through them to find God's hand at work. The story of his life was being written by the invisible hand that is always in control of the story line.

The Palmist said it well:

Do not fret because of evil men or be envious of those who
do wrong; for like the grass they will soon wither, like green
plants they will soon die away. . . . Commit your way to the
Lord; trust in him and he will do this: He will make your
righteousness shine like the dawn, the justice of your cause
like the noonday sun.

Psalms 37:1, 2, 5, 6

Joseph did not doubt that God's hand was at work backstage.
His delight was in being God's man. His way was committed.
There was no need to be anxious.

Second, Joseph did not react with anger. I would have been fu-
rious! I would sure have told Potiphar a thing or two. But Joseph,
like Christ, kept quiet when accused. What would have been
gained by attempting to destroy his superior's wife? Would he
have been better off? Perhaps he would have been worse off.

Again Scripture sets forth its principles: "A fool gives full vent
to his anger, but a wise man keeps himself under control" (Proverbs 29:11). Again it says, "Do not say, 'I'll pay you back for this
wrong!' Wait for the Lord, and he will deliver you. . . . Do not say,
'I'll do to him as he has done to me; I'll pay that man back for
what he did.' . . . Do not repay anyone evil for evil. Be careful to
do what is right in the eyes of everybody" (Proverbs 20:22; 24:29;
Romans 12:17).

We need to weigh our reactions before they're triggered; think
before we speak; be sure our mind is in gear before our mouth is
in motion. We should ask, "Will it make matters worse? Could it
destroy someone else?"

Instead of reacting negatively, Joseph responded with kindness.
He did not implicate his boss's wife. He refused to let it destroy
his trust in God. Further, he continued to serve with excellence. I
dare to believe that he may have prayed for his accuser.

Christ would set forth this very precept later when He said,
"You have heard that it was said, 'Love your neighbor and hate

76

your enemy.' But I tell you: Love your enemies and pray for those who persecute you, that you may be sons of your Father in heaven . . ." (Matthew 5:43–45).

How difficult that is to do. It is so much easier to resent, be bitter, and react. What an example Joseph sets for us.

Furthermore, Joseph did not step in and take charge. Joseph trusted God to settle the score. And indeed he did. He would once again establish Joseph in a far greater position than he had even with Potiphar.

In the end, the final act should be God's. He promises, "A false witness will not go unpunished, and he who pours out lies will perish" (Proverbs 19:9). Again He states, "Do not take revenge, my friends, but leave room for God's wrath, for it is written: 'It is mine to avenge; I will repay,' says the Lord" (Romans 12:19).

Have you taken things out of God's hand and put them in yours? Are you trying to settle the score? As long as you or I do, the score will always remain to our defeat.

Joseph has set the pace for us. He has shown us both what to do and what not to do. Do you feel you are ready to face false accusations? You can be. God eagerly awaits to equip you to handle all of life's adversity.

POINTS TO PONDER

WHO ME? HANDLING UNJUST ACCUSATIONS

1. Does faithfully following God guarantee a trouble-free life? Why or why not?
2. What are the motives mentioned in the chapter for unjust accusations occurring? Can you think of others? What are they?
3. What does Psalm 1 teach about choosing our friendships? Can you apply this successfully to your present friendships?
4. Have you ever been falsely accused? How did you react toward the one making the false accusation? How did you respond to those believing the false accusation?

5
Coping With Life's Prison Experiences

> **MAXIM:**
>
> God doesn't mean for you to live your life imprisoned, but rather empowered.

He had committed murder. At least that's what the phone call indicated. Lonnie was the father of two children who attended our church. The night before, in a drunken stupor, he had allegedly shot and killed his wife and wounded another man. Jealousy had inflamed his actions, and rage had taken control.

Then Lonnie returned to his estranged wife's home and took the two children. Crossing state lines in his flight to avoid arrest, he had committed a federal offense—kidnapping. In just a few hours, his life had exploded in disaster.

The authorities captured Lonnie and took him to the county jail. The caller had asked if I would go visit Lonnie and see if I could be of any help. Immediately a million reasons why I could not go crowded my mind. Important things. I had to trim my mustache. My fingernails were too long and could stand cutting. More importantly, there was a football game on television in ten minutes—so what if the teams were at the bottom of the league battling for the honor of last place!

After sorting through all the critical demands of my life, I realized that none of my excuses would hold water. So off to the jail I drove. I could picture this guy in my mind. I knew he had to be at least 6' 8" and about 240 pounds with hair standing on end as though his finger had been stuck in a light socket. Wild, savage, bloodshot eyes. A sinister snarl on his lips. And worst of all, I knew there must be fangs at the corners of his mouth, with foam oozing out.

Upon arriving at the jail, I was escorted into a visitation cell. What a sound of finality it was to hear the door slam behind me. Shaking (but undoubtedly looking "together" on the outside), I waited. Finally, after an eternity of about four minutes, Lonnie was ushered in.

He stood there, medium height and weight. His appearance was very clean and neat. He wore a sparkling smile. Overall he was a very handsome young man—not at all what I had anticipated.

As we began to talk, Lonnie started to open up concerning his life. The hurt and disappointment came rolling out. The life he described sounded more like a soap opera than reality. A broken marriage. Infidelity. Slavery to alcohol. And that was the tame side.

As the conversation progressed, I was able to share the difference Christ can make in one's life. He asked intelligent questions and made pertinent points. At the end of two hours I found Lonnie praying, asking Christ into his life. Days, months, and years passed. Lonnie was convicted and sent to prison. As I passed through Houston on a trip a few years later, I rented a car and drove to the penitentiary to meet with Lonnie. In our conversation I asked his feelings about being behind bars. His answer is indelibly imprinted upon my mind. "Bob," he stated, "I am freer inside these bars than many people who are on the other side of them. Though I am incarcerated physically, many of them are in prisons far more terrible than mine. I know one day I will be released. Some of the people on the outside may never escape from their own prisons."

Driving away from that penal institution, his words reverberated in my mind. I knew that he had made one of the deepest philosophical statements I would ever hear. My mind leaped back to the story of Joseph. Life had seemed to be on the upswing but suddenly Joseph was to find himself in a prison. Unlike Lonnie, Joseph found himself imprisoned on trumped-up charges. Nevertheless, he experienced freedom in the midst of life's prison experience. Joseph found that one can be in limiting circumstances and yet remain liberated.

As I watch people around me moving freely, I cannot help but wonder how many of them are peering out from bars of internment. Many are silently immobilized and passive in life's journey. Rather than a joyful experience, life becomes a drudgery of bondage.

Prison comes in different forms for different people.

Circumstances. Many find themselves in circumstances which seem to hinder their fulfillment in life. Nothing seems to be right. A grass-is-greener syndrome begins to permeate their minds.

While living in Florida, I had the privilege of directing the National Training Ministry for a rapidly growing Christian organization. My responsibilities allowed me to speak and teach all across the country. As I would be introduced before speaking, the master of ceremonies would inevitably mention that I lived in Ft. Lauderdale. This happened in Seattle, Washington, and following my message, a man came up and said, "So you're from Ft. Lauderdale! I wish I could live down there. Things just aren't going well for me here. But if I could be there, I'm convinced that my problems would be solved and my life changed. The circumstances here just aren't right."

A few days later, I returned home. Since I had been gone for some time, my yard needed attention. Donning my bathing suit, I went out to practice the fine art of horticulture. To my surprise, one of my neighbors was also home that weekday working in his yard. With a friendly wave I greeted him and asked him how things were going. He shrugged and asked me where I had been. When I mentioned Seattle, his response stopped me dead in my tracks. "So you've been to Seattle, huh? I'd love to be in Seattle. Things just aren't going very well for me here, but I bet if I was in a place like that, things would be going great."

I had to burst out in an unexpected fit of laughter. I'm sure that he still to this day doesn't know what I saw so funny in his comments. But the response depicts many of us very well. We always think that a change in circumstances will be the answer for every challenge we face.

How different is that type of outlook from Paul's when he said, "Give thanks in all circumstances, for this is God's will for you in Christ Jesus" (1 Thessalonians 5:18). When we allow circumstances to master us rather than seeing that the Master is in charge of our circumstances, we become imprisoned.

Others' expectations. Several years ago Harvard psychologist Robert Rosenthal performed an intriguing experiment regarding performance of children based on the teacher's expectations. He hoped to prove that raising the teacher's expectations would raise the children's performance as well. So Rosenthal tested a group of children and assigned them at random to teachers who thought they were exceptional students since they were labeled as "spurters."

At the end of the school year, the children were tested once again and the results were astounding. They gained as many as fifteen to twenty-seven I.Q. points as a direct result of the teacher's attitude toward them. Because the teachers expected more out of these "spurters," the children came to expect more of themselves.

My wife, who is wonderful with children, saw this principle manifested in her early teaching career. Cheryl was assigned to a low income school in the city of Dallas. The school was heavily populated with minority children. One of the little girls in her class by the name of Julie was reported to be a real troublemaker. As she had been described by the other teachers, Cheryl began to expect the worst from Julie. To say that things didn't go well would be a gross understatement.

In reflecting upon an unusually difficult time with Julie, Cheryl began to look for creative ways in which she might be able to influence Julie's actions. The school administration was encouraging teachers to establish positive communication with the home when possible.

One day Julie went out of her way to help my wife accomplish a task in class, which was a rather rare event for the child. Cheryl sat down and wrote a very gracious note to the mother, complimenting and praising Julie for what she had done in class. The change was incredible! It was as though Julie had suddenly become "clothed and in her right mind." She became a sweet, supportive, and cooperative student.

Finally, not being able to stand the suspense any longer, Cheryl asked Julie to stop by her desk following class. She asked Julie what had been responsible for the change, and the young lady displayed a huge grin and said, "Your note to my mother. You told my mother that you thought I was special and could be a big help. And I want to be just the way you expect me to be."

Goethe, the famous German writer, said, "Treat people as if

they are what they ought to be and you will help them become what they are capable of becoming." Many people today are imprisoned because of the views or expectations of other people. What's worse, perhaps many of us put others "in prison" by the expectations we force upon them.

Lack of confidence. Henry Ford said, "Think you can, think you can't; either way you are right." Too many of us are walking around with a defeated attitude. We feel we cannot make a meaningful contribution or accomplish a meaningful task. Fear of taking risks paralyzes us. We do not see ourselves adequate for the tasks before us. James Bryant Conant, the distinguished president of Harvard, challenged us all when he said, "Behold the turtle—he makes progress only when he sticks his neck out." Yet, we tuck in our necks and seek only to be comfortable.

Where would we be today in travel had the Wright brothers never risked the maiden voyage at Kitty Hawk? Or how would you race to the store on a quick errand had Henry Ford let bankruptcy stop him? Had Reggie Jackson been unwilling to risk a second year in the majors after an embarrassing rookie season, we would never have known the great batting king whom we praise today. The fear of failure handcuffs more people than any other condition in our time.

Guilt. Many of us walk around with a heavy burden on our shoulders labeled "guilt." Acts or circumstances from even many years before continue as a haunting refrain in our conscience. Though others may have forgiven us, often the problem is that we have not forgiven ourselves.

Perhaps the worse type of guilt is false guilt. Many times this is imposed upon us by others and is generated by a cultural Christianity. Too often people sit under a Christianity which has been reduced to a list of do's and don'ts (with emphasis on the don'ts). The list has become too staggering to bear. Many of the "rules" were not even biblically based. As a result, people walk hunched over from the weight of man-imposed guidelines.

Loneliness. Today the average American meets as many people in one year as the average person did in a lifetime seventy-five years ago. And yet, today, he is far lonelier. This does not necessarily mean that he is alone, for loneliness can happen in the very midst of a great crowd. Yet psychologists tell us that possibly the largest struggle battering down the doors of people's lives presently is the threat of loneliness. Dr. Leonard Cammer, a psychiatrist who dealt with depressed people for over thirty years, said, "The human being is the only species that can't survive alone. The human being needs another human being—otherwise he's dead!"

Perhaps one of the greatest difficulties contributing to loneliness is the lack of healthy self-worth. Too much emphasis has been placed on the shallow facade of bucks, beauty, and brains. When we look in the mirror and don't match the jet-setters and role models displayed on television and plastered in magazines, we feel as though we just can't measure up. Nobody wants to be with us.

The problem is that we have established the measure of self-worth in the wrong things. Beauty, brains, and bucks are not the answer. Instead, if you had to place a price tag on your life, the only true inscription would be "Jesus Christ." He sees you as being of such worth that He gave His life on the cross for you. It has nothing to do with whether you fit the mold of the "successful" person. It has everything to do with the fact that you are God's creation. Therefore, your self-worth is based on the fact that you are a uniquely created individual. There's not another person like you anywhere. God thought you were so special that He paid the price of Jesus Christ, His Son, to allow you to reach all the potential with which you were created.

Pessimism. Many of us are walking through life imprisoned with an outlook that expects the worse. We are like the man who wore an emergency bracelet inscribed with these words: "In case of accident . . . I'm not surprised!" When we move through life expecting the worst, we will usually find it.

Regardless of what "prison experience" we may find ourselves facing, Joseph can provide us with insights for coping. It is important as we look at his circumstances to remember that he was human as we are. To think he went into incarceration with a silly pious grin on his face is ridiculous. We must imagine some of the feelings he must have felt.

First, he would have felt abandoned. He had given himself fully to his job. As estate administrator for Potiphar, he had not only proved to be an excellent executive, but Joseph also established himself as an outstandingly ethical person. No doubt he had been surrounded by people who answered directly to him. Due to Potiphar's position, the estate was a very large one and this responsibility great. Now Joseph found himself totally abandoned in a dark, dank cell.

When we find ourselves in the midst of a prison experience in life, we most often feel abandoned. It seems as though no one cares. They don't have time for us. At times they don't even seem to realize that we exist.

Second, Joseph felt a sense of doom. The charges had been serious. Undoubtedly he knew he had narrowly escaped death. The law in Egypt for such a crime as Joseph had been accused would have been death. Perhaps the fact that he found himself in prison was an indication that Potiphar did not totally believe his wife's story.

Regardless of the facts, for all Joseph knew he could rot in this prison. Hope would have been a difficult thing to grasp. Light at the end of the tunnel seemed all but extinguished.

So it is with us. When life closes in, we feel as though there is no escape. Circumstances become a trap rather than a means to fulfillment.

Third, Joseph most probably felt forgotten. Regardless of his loyal service and outstanding track record, no one seemed to remember where he was. Visitors were probably few, if any. On top of that, perhaps even God had forgotten him. Those thoughts most surely must have gone through his mind. He would have well identified with David of later years, who said, "Save me, O God, for the waters have come up to my neck. I sink in the miry depths, where there is no foothold. I have come into the deep waters; the floods engulf me. I am worn out calling for help; my throat is parched. My eyes fail, looking for my God" (Psalms 69:1–3).

One of the things we must keep in mind as we look at Joseph is that *God is not as much interested in our circumstances as in our response to circumstances.* Modeling after Joseph's responses can be a great training ground regardless of what circumstances you may face. For it is in your response that God is able to establish the firmness of your faith as well as the purity of your motives.

Joseph Kept a Proper Perspective

In the midst of the normal human feelings resulting from imprisonment, Joseph realized the importance of perspective. How we view situations determines our perspective of them. As a result, it is important that our eyes are focused on the problem correctly. We must avoid becoming introspective in our circumstances. When we allow our vision to center on ourselves in our seeming prison, self-pity quickly follows in its wake.

How easy it would have been for Joseph to feel sorry for himself. After all, he had given it his best shot. He had been faithful to his superior and his integrity had seen him through temptation. He had already bounced back from one devastating blow to his life only to find himself abandoned, doomed, and forgotten once more.

When self-pity is allowed to take root, a terrible condition usually follows. I call it the "comfort in sickness" syndrome. Have you ever noticed that when you are ill and feeling so terrible, you find it nice to have someone wait on you? When you need something to drink or medicine, it's nice to call for someone to bring it to you. When you need help moving around, how comforting it is to have someone there to support you. When you want the television turned on or off, someone usually becomes your remote control.

As the days go by, it is easy to find ourselves almost dreading to get well. After all, it's been nice being waited on. The attention has been grand. Perhaps being sick isn't all that bad. Perspective has become inwardly directed. So it is with some who find themselves in the prison experiences of life. Self-pity has taken hold and soon they are not even sure they want out. They are getting a lot of attention and sympathy. The more they get, the more they tend to feed upon it. Rather than make efforts at finding a way out of the prison, they snuggle down in the corner of their cell, waiting for the next kind soul to come and minister to them.

Joseph kept his perspective. He kept the vision of his spirit directed to the God who was in control. Though outward circumstances seemed to devastate all hope, Joseph continued to trust in the God of circumstances. With Paul, Joseph could say, ". . . I have learned to be content whatever the circumstances. I know what it is to be in need, and I know what it is to have plenty. I have learned the secret of being content in any and every situation, whether well fed or hungry, whether living in plenty or in want. I can do everything through him who gives me strength" (Philippians 4:11–13).

In your present situation, how is your perspective? Has it become inwardly directed? Or are you able to trust God's sovereignty in every situation? Could it be possible that you are a little mad at God? Then you need to hear Isaiah's warning: "Woe to him who quarrels with his Maker, to him who is but a potsherd among the potsherds on the ground. Does the clay say to the potter, 'What are you making?' Does your work say, 'He has no hands'?" (Isaiah 45:9.) Be careful lest in your prison you find yourself striving with sovereignty!

Joseph Maintained a Proper Priority

Had Joseph allowed his perspective to center upon himself, he would have found himself unaware not only of God but of others. Prison experiences often stifle your concern for others. This was not the case with Joseph. Even in the midst of adversity, he reached out to help others. As a result, the Bible tells us, "The warden put Joseph in charge of all those held in the prison, and he was made responsible for all that was done there. The warden paid no attention to anything under Joseph's care, because the Lord was with Joseph and gave him success in whatever he did" (Genesis 39:22, 23).

During his imprisonment, Joseph was to meet the king's cupbearer and baker. These were trusted officials of Pharaoh's court. The chief cupbearer had the responsibility of tasting all the food and drink before Pharaoh ate any meal. If he lived, the Pharaoh felt free to enjoy the meal; if he died . . . oh well, time for another cupbearer. The baker had the responsibility of cooking the food for his sovereign. Scripture does not tell us why they were thrown in prison, only that they became co-inmates with Joseph. Whatever happened, it must have been extremely serious to have both of these trusted members of the court imprisoned.

How easy it would have been for Joseph to feel "It serves you right. If I am here, then I'm glad you are here too." Instead we find no such attitude. When both the cupbearer and baker had dreams, Joseph gave himself away in ministry to them. First he interpreted their dreams as God gave him the insight to do. For the cupbearer it would be the good news of eventual release. For the chief baker, however, it would be news of ultimate execution. Joseph's ministry to each man was characterized by openness and honesty.

As He journeyed to Jerusalem just before His crucifixion, Jesus could have thought only about Himself. Yet Scripture tells us the opposite occurred. Going into Jericho, he met a blind man by the name of Bartimaeus. While the crowd and disciples encouraged him to move on quickly, He stopped and granted Bartimaeus what he wished for most—his sight.

Traveling on through the city, Jesus came to a man who was experiencing his own prison. Zacchaeus was a chief tax collector. Though he was wealthy and had all that he could want, he lacked the most important thing in life—friends. He had bid against his own countrymen to collect taxes for the Roman government. He was allowed to collect as much as he could get away with. Anything over and above what the Roman government required was his to keep. Deceit and cheating was a way of life for him. As a result, his life was in constant danger.

To this "up and out" man Jesus stopped and ministered. As a result of His reaching out and touching the life of Zacchaeus, the tax collector's life was never the same. There was a radical change in both his own life and his perspective toward others.

What must be remembered in this event is the drama Jesus had facing Him in the immediate future. How easy it would have been for Him to have retreated in a prison of fear, dread, or self-pity. But we find none of those evidenced here. Even in the midst of difficult times, Jesus maintained a proper priority by giving Himself away to others.

Joseph, like Jesus after him, focused on others' needs before his own. He had come to realize the truth: that in giving ourselves away, we actually find ourselves. The greatest gift that any of us can give is not money or things but ourselves.

Joseph Experienced a Perfect Peace

Even in Joseph's incarceration, Scripture gives no indication of bitterness, resentment, or worry on his behalf. Though he did not have Scripture to read at that point, he understood the spiritual principle of the New Testament. "Do not be anxious about anything, but in everything, by prayer and petition, with thanksgiving, present your requests to God. And the peace of God, which transcends all understanding, will guard your hearts and your minds in Christ Jesus" (Philippians 4:6, 7). Joseph must have realized that worry can be debilitating. Thus he had made his request known to God. Surely he wanted release. Most probably his prayers daily asked God for deliverance. But even in the midst of continued difficult circumstances, peace pervaded his life. Joseph realized that even in the midst of prison experiences, God was accomplishing His purpose.

The same God who delivered Joseph from the pit was able to deliver him from prison. Yet even with this peace, we find Joseph requesting the help of another in his possible release. In Genesis 40:14 Joseph had asked the cupbearer to remember him and his kindness by mentioning his situation to the Pharaoh. Like any of us, he wanted out. Asking others for help is perfectly acceptable. They may possibly be the instruments that God will use to release us from our dilemma. However, the final deliverance will be accomplished by God Himself. And in that fact, Joseph had peace even when the chief cupbearer failed to remember him.

Though Joseph did not have the luxury of reading Philippians 4:6, 7, he undoubtedly had the "peace of God." Because Joseph was at peace *with* his Creator by being in right relationship with Him and obedient to God's leadership in his life, he was able to experience the peace *of* God.

Joseph Exhibited a Positive Attitude

How well we would understand Joseph if anger and frustration arose in him at being forgotten. Yet we find no evidence of this. He maintained the posture of serving faithfully, keeping his eyes on God, and remaining in perfect peace. I've become convinced as I watch people that 90 percent of how we feel is determined by our attitudes. Circumstances may change and vary but our attitude makes or breaks our environment.

Recently a young man crossed my path who has made a dynamic impact on my life. In 1981 Kevin Neal was playing with his Big Wheel on the driveway of his home. Inadvertently Kevin gained speed, rapidly going down the inclined drive, and flashed in front of a passing car. The resulting collision left Kevin hanging onto life by a mere thread. His small body lay crumpled in a hospital bed. Days led into months. Hope threatened to flee.

Then a miracle occurred. Kevin began to respond. And since that time, he has made phenomenal gains. He is able to walk with the aid of a walker or cane. Recently, he took his first steps unassisted.

During the time I've known Kevin, the one amazing thing that has stood out in his character is his attitude. Surrounded by a prison of physical impairment and struggling with the inability to run and play with his friends, Kevin continues to exhibit a positive "can do" attitude. You never have to wonder what Kevin's answer will be when he is asked how he's doing. "Fine!" will be the immediate reply. What's more, he will always ask you how you are doing. Kevin personifies the truth that attitude makes the difference in a life that is beset by problems and difficulties.

While conducting a service recently I extended a public invitation to those willing to commit to the Lord's service. Several came. As I heard a rustling down one of the aisles, I looked up and was captivated by what I saw. Struggling and with faltering steps, Kevin was making his way to the front. Some of the young people in our church walked beside him to help steady his steps. As Kevin reached me, he said that he wasn't sure exactly what he could do for the Lord, but he wanted to do everything possible. He wanted his life to count. As a result, it was as though the floodgates opened. Many people responded that morning because they saw one far less fortunate than they who had the courage and the positive attitude to make the best of the situation.

How are you doing in your situation? Are you like Kevin, making the best of the circumstances in which you find yourself? Your attitude will greatly determine the outcome of your present circumstances.

Joseph Exuded a Patient Demeanor

Joseph patiently waited on the Lord for his deliverance. For the contemporary man, patience is a difficult concept with which to struggle. In our instant society of microwave ovens, microchip computers, and millisecond transmission of information, we do not like to wait. We look for patience as some gift-wrapped package that God drops in our laps at the mere asking.

Unfortunately, patience is born and refined in the crucible of difficult circumstances. It is actually in wading through the deep waters that we gain the patience we so sorely need.

Waiting is not our strong suit. Yet Scripture says it is one of the endearing characteristics of the man or woman who follows God. The writer of Proverbs said, "Man's wisdom gives him patience . . ." (Proverbs 19:11). The Psalmist says, "Wait for the Lord; be strong and take heart and wait for the Lord" (Psalms 27:14). Isaiah made a similar comment: "Yet the Lord longs to be gracious to you; he rises to show you compassion. For the Lord is a God of justice. Blessed are all who wait for him!" (Isaiah 30:18.)

Joseph realized two great principles of patiently waiting for God's move in the midst of our trials. First, he recalled:

God's timing will always be such that it will show our inadequacy in an impossible situation.

In his prison cell there was nothing Joseph could do to extricate himself. The possibility of freedom seemed nonexistent. It is in these very times that God moves. God's confidence begins at the end of self-confidence.

Second, young Joseph saw that God was adequate for every circumstance and situation:

God's timing will always be such that it will show His adequacy in impossible situations.

It has been that way throughout history. God has never promised to remove all the obstacles but instead to give us what is needed to cope with them. To the Apostle Paul He never promised to remove the problems, but instead said, "My grace is sufficient for you . . ." (2 Corinthians 12:9).

Third, Joseph must have realized:

God's timing will always be such that He will get the greatest glory.

Many times our desires are for God to meet our timetable of events. But He will always wait until He knows that His name will be most highly exalted. This was beautifully illustrated through the life of Jesus. His dear friend Lazarus lay on his deathbed. Mary and Martha, his sisters, urgently sent for Christ saying, "Lord, the one you love is sick" (John 11:3).

Our immediate expectation would be that upon receiving the news, Jesus would have made haste to Bethany to heal His friend. But this was not to be. In fact Jesus delayed two more days before going. Why? Jesus Himself gave the answer: "This sickness will not end in death. No, it is for God's glory so that God's Son may be glorified through it" (John 11:4).

Perhaps you are waiting for God to move but if He were to do so immediately, you or someone else would receive the glory. He will wait until He knows His name will be glorified in the solution of the problem. Be patient. Be assured God is at work.

Perhaps the final lesson you should keep in mind is that impossible situations may not be impossible at all. There is no prison lock that God is not capable of picking. He is the Master escape artist. And He doesn't need your help. All He needs is your openness and submission.

Perhaps you keep your God much too small. If you find yourself imprisoned, you feel that He must be limited as well. But thank God, He is not limited to your dimensions or circumstances. There is another entire world that is invisible—the spiritual world—in which He reigns supreme! And *He is able!*

I believe Chuck Swindoll says it well: "We are all faced with a series of great opportunities brilliantly disguised as impossible situations." But remember, nothing is impossible with God. With His divine intervention, no prison cell will ever hold you. But like Joseph . . . and Peter . . . and Paul, it will probably take God to release you from your prison experience. As you wait for His timing, allow Him to empower you to deal with the circumstances in which you find yourself. For remember, your circumstances will never make or break you; instead, you will make or break your circumstances.

POINTS TO PONDER

COPING WITH LIFE'S PRISON EXPERIENCES

1. Recall some of the ways mentioned in the chapter in which people can find themselves "imprisoned" in life. Have you known anyone imprisoned by some of these things?

2. How did Joseph respond to his imprisonment? Imagine yourself in his shoes. How do you think you would have responded?

3. Why is it so easy to have your perspective become self-centered in the midst of adversity? How do you prevent this?

4. What was Joseph's view of God in the midst of adversity? What do you normally find yours to be? If there is a difference, what do you think is the reason?

5. In your own words, distinguish the difference between "peace *with* God" and "the peace *of* God."

6. We looked at three principles of waiting found in Joseph's life. Practically apply these three principles to the most recent experience of waiting you have had.

6
The
Waiting Rooms
of Life

MAXIM:

When life is in a holding pattern, it's not how long you wait that is important, it's how you wait for whatever length of time.

Have you ever noticed that rooms speak for themselves? Walk into a freshly decorated nursery prepared by proud expectant parents. Immediately the room speaks of joy, excitement, and anticipation. It proclaims the coming of happy days!

Enter into a cozy den on a cold winter evening. A large fire is roaring in the fireplace, casting a gentle hue upon the room's contents. In the dim light shadows dance in syncopated time with the crackling of the fire. Gentle easy-listening music floats through the air from the quadraphonic sound system. The room offers a gracious invitation to come in, sit down, and be enveloped by its atmosphere.

Or walk into a festively appointed dining room during the holiday season. Plates at each chair wait to hold a sumptuous feast. Down the hall, the sound of friendly voices and the warmth of laughter drift through the air. The room sings the theme of celebration and the reunion of friends and relatives.

But other rooms are not nearly so inviting. Some rooms are lonely regardless of the number of people within them. Discouragement reigns. A frightened uncertainty prevails. These are the waiting rooms.

In my daily routine I have the opportunity often to be in the waiting rooms of medical institutions. There I watch people experiencing the full range of human emotions. The waiting rooms of life are difficult and challenging to cope with and yet, throughout our journey in "this land below," life brings us so many experiences which develop into "waiting rooms."

Perhaps you are waiting to launch into a new arena of education. Or, perhaps you are finished with education and are waiting the notification of new employment. Maybe the wait is for children. Or, having children, maybe you are waiting for them to grow up and leave home, launching into the journey of their own adulthood. Or could it be that your wait is for next year, or a long-dreamed-about trip; maybe you find yourself just waiting to die.

These waiting periods are difficult to deal with. We are unaccustomed to waiting. We live in an instamatic society. Our telephones are touchtone. Our ovens are microwave. Our information is generated on a computer screen at the touch of a keyboard. With this life-style, who wants to wait?

It is here that Joseph again teaches us a critical insight to successful living. He too was faced with a "waiting room." Having been imprisoned on false charges, deliverance was not quick in coming. As we saw in the last chapter, he met the Pharaoh's chief baker and chief cupbearer, who had also been incarcerated. He had interpreted their dreams. It had been good news and bad news. For the chief cupbearer, the interpretation brought the good news of release and being restored to his former position. The bad news was that the chief baker got no good news at all. For him the dream's interpretation called for execution.

Hoping to see light at the end of the tunnel, Joseph had requested the cupbearer to remember him and his plight to Pharaoh (Genesis 40:14). But as so often happens when we are in a period of waiting, things don't work out according to our wishes. And so, things had not worked out the way Joseph had hoped. It was as though he had never existed. No one remembered him. He must have felt like a man captured in a time warp in which days lost meaning. His life had been put into a low-altitude holding pattern for two years. Surely there must have been days on which he felt he was running out of fuel. I can identify with this man, can't you?

Suddenly the holding pattern was interrupted. The day began not unlike the previous 712 days. It was just another day in the dungeon. The normal doldrums were jolted by a dilemma. Pharaoh had a dream. Actually he had two dreams.

These dreams were not your garden-variety type. In the first one, seven fat cows were devoured by seven ghastly and gaunt cows. In the second dream, seven picture-perfect ears of grain were swallowed up by seven that were scorched and dry. All the king's horses and all the king's men—Pharaoh's magicians and counselors—came before the shattered and shocked Pharaoh. Try as they may, it seemed they could not interpret his dream and thus were unable to "put Humpty Dumpty together again." Though skilled and educated, they were short on wisdom and understanding.

Suddenly the cupbearer "happened" to remember Joseph.

Telling Pharaoh of Joseph's ability to interpret the cupbearer's dream in prison, he must have seen Pharaoh's eyes lighten with hope. Joseph was immediately summoned. He had moved from the pit to the pinnacle in one quick step. The time of waiting in the stone-cold dungeon had finally expired. He had been in Egypt for thirteen long years. His arduous ordeal had put him to the test, but he had passed with flying colors.

Though Joseph was not as fortunate as we are in having the revealed counsel of God, he seemed to intuitively sense principles for godly living, including the principles for coping with periods of waiting. These principles, still valid today, will help us deal with those difficult times in life in which we find ourselves in a holding pattern.

Wait Alertly

During waiting periods, we need to be especially sensitive to God's intentions and actions. The writer of Proverbs says, "Blessed is the man who listens to me, watching daily at my doors, waiting at my doorway" (8:34). Though waiting may seem passive to many, it should actually be active. You cannot effectively wait by simply resting on your laurels. Instead, you must be alertly tuned to God's intentions.

Quite often in the waiting rooms of life God prepares us for what is coming. If these waiting times are docilely endured, valuable time can be wasted. As the Scripture indicates, we are to be *listening* and *watching* during these times. This requires active concentration and attention.

In the desert experiences of my own life, I have found that I need to ask myself two questions:

1. Is there something God is trying to teach me during this time of waiting?

2. Is there something God is attempting to change in my life during this time of waiting?

These two questions have often brought me face-to-face with a fresh touch of God's hand in my life. Before this became a reality to me, I wasted many waiting rooms. I have too often been distracted by the superficial and thus missed the supernatural. He has promised that as He directs our lives, He will give counsel. The purpose of counsel is always to give insight and directives so that the one receiving them can live life to the maximum. What a tragedy it is when we miss those opportunities of waiting alertly.

It would seem that Joseph knew how to wait with the ears of his heart open. For him, waiting was nothing to be shrugged off. Instead it would seem he was alert, looking for God's hand and direction.

Waiting can be the training ground in which we are molded to become more like God. In waiting, we can develop hearts that are sensitive to Him. When things are going well, we seem to have little need to trust and rely upon the Father. Yet, in waiting we become keenly aware of our need.

It is also true, however, that at such times our Adversary moves in quickly with attacks of doubt. God warns us to "be self-controlled and alert. Your enemy the devil prowls around like a roaring lion looking for someone to devour. Resist him, standing firm in the faith . . ." (1 Peter 5:8, 9). So we will make the decision to be alert or dulled. We will draw close to the Lord or we will drift from Him. We will resist the devil's attacks of doubt, anger, and frustration or we will give them a foothold on the beachhead of our lives. But whatever the outcome, it will directly result from our free choice.

Wait Expectantly

Have you ever waited for something you really desired and just "knew it would happen any time"? Then as days and weeks passed, your expectancy began to dwindle. Expectancy then changed to drudgery. Soon questions arose as to whether the hope or dream would ever occur.

I remember once in graduate school when a great opportunity must have turned the wrong corner. Hope and excitement began to disintegrate into despair.

I well remember one evening sitting on the porch of our apartment, wondering where God was. I felt I had been so faithful and worked hard. Why weren't things coming together? After all, hadn't God said He would "give us the desires of our heart"?

Then I discovered a portion of Scripture. The Psalmist wrote, "I wait for the Lord, my soul waits, and in his word I put my hope. My soul waits for the Lord more than watchmen wait for the morning, more than watchmen wait for the morning" (Psalms 130:5, 6). The biblical writer said he was waiting and putting his hope in God's Word. Honest self-evaluation forced me to admit that the longer the wait became, the less commitment I had to being in God's Word. Yet, the Psalmist wrote that he was able to count on God fulfilling His Word even more than the watchmen could expect the sunrise of the morning. Determining in my mind that sunrise was a fairly trustworthy occurrence, I was driven back to the basics: either I trusted God and His Word or I didn't. I was reminded that waiting can either draw one to God or drive one away from God.

To put one's hope in God and His Word is more than mere wistful longing. Hope used in Scripture most often refers to the expectation of good and deliverance. Hebrews tells us that "faith is being sure of what we hope for and certain of what we do not see" (11:1). To live with that type of faith is to have such an expectation of God's grace and goodness that it gives absolute assurance regardless of circumstances. Biblical hope is the most solid ground on which to stand. It is the conviction that God will do as He says.

Where do we get that type of hope? Scripture has the answer. "For everything that was written in the past was written to teach us, so that through endurance and the encouragement of the Scriptures we might have hope" (Romans 15:4). When endurance and patience are required, the encouragement that comes from the Scriptures brings hope. As God's faithfulness is repeatedly seen, hope springs anew. Circumstances become secondary and God's faithfulness becomes primary. As a result, expectation increases.

When the Lord is trusted expectantly, Isaiah 40:31 becomes reality. It is then that the Lord renews our strength. As our confidence shifts from the hope that "things will work out" to the "God who works all things out," we experience renewal internally. Our spirit begins to soar as on wings of eagles.

That sounds almost poetic, doesn't it? To soar with wings like eagles? But before you start feeling cozy and warm, have you ever stopped to analyze how eagles learn to soar? It's not an easy or enjoyable process. Before the eaglets are hatched, the mother lines the nest with soft animal fur and grass. As they begin to mature, the eaglets nestle in the comfort and warmth of their "home, sweet home."

It is not long, however, before they begin to flex their muscles. Mother realizes they have advanced to a new stage of development and opportunity. The time for nestling in comfort is gone. Almost ruthlessly she begins to rip away the soft lining of the nest. What had been a comfortable lounging area becomes a devilish tangle of thorns, broken sticks, and branches. It is the last place anyone would want to stay and relax. The motivation is outstanding for fostering the desire to go on to the next stage of development.

It is then that the mother grabs an eaglet in her talons and soars to the heights. Amazing things must cross the eaglet's mind as it gets a bird's-eye view from heights it has never previously experienced. Suddenly, the mother's talons loosen and the eaglet begins to plummet to earth. Can you imagine the sheer panic?

Just when it seems that all hope is lost, the mother swoops

under the eaglet, catching it on her powerful and broad shoulders. The racing heartbeat calms as security is once again restored. Surely they must now be headed back to the comfort of the nest. But alas, the mother once again soars to heights above. Unexpectedly, she dips her shoulder and the eaglet begins to flutter downward once more.

Finally, after several of these wild and crazy experiments, the wings begin to function. The air currents course over their leading edge. As the strong feathered armatures catch the moving air, the eaglet begins to hold himself aloft. Soon it is not only flying, but soaring on the warm thermals.

How similarly God treats you and me. He allows us to move, and sometimes fall, through the unknown. We anxiously wait for Him to deliver. Sometimes it is not as quick as we would hope. Once deliverance comes, it does not prove to be a once-for-all experience. There will come a time when we again find ourselves waiting for His rescue. All the while, He is forcing us to use our spiritual wings. It is in that process that the Lord renews our strength. It is then that even in the midst of waiting, we may run with busy schedules and yet not grow weary. We may walk through the routines of daily living and not faint.

I believe Joseph waited expectantly. He knew that the God who had given him the dream of a destiny would fulfill it. He expected good and deliverance. And so it would become reality.

Wait Quietly and Patiently

My father-in-law knows me well. A few years ago he purchased a plaque for my study. On it was what I call the American prayer: "Lord grant me patience ... and grant it to me now!" Many of us have trouble being quiet and patient. Yet these are critical ingredients of effective waiting.

Scripture tells us, "The Lord is good to those whose hope is in him, to the one who seeks him; it is good to wait quietly for the salvation of the Lord" (Lamentations 3:25, 26). Have you ever noticed how hard it is for people to wait quietly? Let there be a long line waiting for concert tickets and you find the longer people wait, the louder they become. Let motorists have to wait through two or three changes of a traffic signal and the horns begin to blare. We complain vehemently when we're put on hold on the telephone.

It has always amazed me that when God led the children of Israel into the Promised Land, He gave them an interesting strategy for conquering Jericho. As you well remember, they were to march around the city once daily for six days. On the seventh day they were to march around seven times, sound the trumpets and shout, and the walls were promised to tumble down. Yet I find that the most interesting ingredient is that they were instructed not to talk at all during those seven days. Have you ever wondered why?

In studying their history, I think I have an idea why God instructed them to wait quietly as they followed His plan for those seven days. Prior to that time when God had moved in a miraculous way to deliver them, they had been thankful—for a few hours, days, or weeks. This would then be followed by their facing a new trial of some type. It seems that they would quickly forget how God had provided for them in the recent past. Soon you would hear, "Murmur, murmur, murmur, murmur . . . complain, complain, complain." This cycle was repeated over and over again.

Do you remember the details? After 430 years in bondage, God had released Israel from Egypt. Moses led them as they fled. A cloud led them by day and a pillar of fire by night. As they came to the Red Sea, they heard the thundering of approaching hoofbeats. The Egyptians, realizing their mistake in letting their free labor escape, were in hot pursuit. What did Israel do? They immediately began to complain and murmur.

With a trumpeting call, Moses challenged them to stand firm

and see God's deliverance. Sure enough, God opened the sea for Israel to cross on dry land. As soon as they were safe and the Egyptians were in the midst of the sea, He let it close upon the enemy, destroying the pursuing army.

Shortly thereafter Israel came to the water at Marah. Thirsty, they began to gulp down the water only to find that it was very bitter. And what did they do? Complained and grumbled! Even despite their weak faith, God turned the water into a sweet and cooling liquid. He then took them on to the oasis of Elim, an answer better than they had hoped for.

But that memory didn't last long either. Having been filled with water, they became hungry. And, you guessed it, they began to complain and murmur.

Their murmuring reached the sensitive ears of God. Regardless of how many times He had moved in their favor, they seemed not to be appreciative of what they had. And so, being a giving God, He provided them with something to put in their stomachs. A wafer-type substance called "manna" served as their bread. And then He gave them something to put on the bread, fresh quail. Not only did God provide them both manna and quail, but it was an all-you-can-eat smorgasbord.

But it wasn't long until Israel was complaining again. After all that to eat, they were thirsty. And so God provided them with fresh water, this time from a rock. Again and again He showed He could meet whatever need they had in a most incredible and unexpected way. But somehow it never seemed to sink in.

Could it be that one of the reasons God emphasizes being quiet before Him is that He knows our tendency? Is it also the very reason He asked the children of Israel to march quietly around Jericho? He knew that if they talked, they would end up complaining and murmuring. It seems that if we also don't practice disciplining and controlling our tongues, we can easily, like Israel, end up murmuring and complaining. We must put a guard at our lips. It is that staunch sentinel that allows us to sometimes hear God more clearly. How many times have you and I missed God's voice and message because we were too busy complaining and murmuring? Maybe we should spend more time recounting in our memories how God has provided in the past and less time complaining and murmuring about the present circumstances. This is true even when the present circumstances rage like a hurricane around us.

While living in Florida, I became fascinated with hurricanes. I well remember when Hurricane David was racing toward the coast of Ft. Lauderdale. Warnings blanketed our city, and everyone began to prepare for potential disaster. Lines at the stores seemed to wind unendingly from the cash registers. People stocked up on every commodity which would be needed should the worst occur. Glass windows were taped and braced to withstand the coming winds.

As the winds began to make the trees outside of our home dance like marionettes, I tuned in to the weather reports. Listening attentively, I heard that the Coast Guard was helping keep track of the hurricane. The weather announcer explained that though winds may race over a hundred miles per hour along the edge of the hurricane, the center or the "eye" is very calm. It is so calm and peaceful that a plane can fly around inside it for some time with no turbulence.

As I listened, I thought how like God is the center of a hurricane. Though life may be swirling around us at an incredible pace, God's presence can bring an unearthly quietness. It is only in spending time with Him that the frantic winds of life become still. Have you tried letting Him be the eye of your storm?

Along with quiet waiting, we must wait patiently. Again the biblical writer instructs us to come "be still before the Lord and wait patiently for him . . ." (Psalms 37:7). Unfortunately patience is a commodity in short supply. The word most often used in Scripture for *patience* is a word that means "to abide under." It means that we are unwilling to surrender and collapse when under trying circumstances. This "abiding under" can have both a passive and active quality.

The active quality as used in Scripture indicates pressing on despite obstacles that may be faced. It portrays an active determination not to give in—not to falter from exhaustion or difficulty. This is what the writer of Hebrews meant when he said, ". . . let us run with *perseverance* the race marked out for us. Let us fix our eyes on Jesus, the author and perfecter of our faith . . ." (12:1, 2, *italics mine*). It is the picture not of the sprinter, but of the distance runner. Even when his body cries out from seeming fatigue, his mind does not give in. He instructs his body to keep running the race set before him. So it is with us as we run the race of life. God calls us to press on.

But once we have done all we can, we must also trust God to accomplish His purposes. This more passive posture is often referred to as endurance. Romans 12:12 uses it when it says, "Be joyful in hope, *patient* in affliction, faithful in prayer" (*italics mine*). Paul uses it in 2 Timothy when he cries, "Therefore, I endure everything for the sake of the elect, that they too may obtain the salvation that is in Christ Jesus, with eternal glory . . . if we endure, we will also reign with him . . ." (2:10, 12).

In waiting patiently both the active and the passive elements are involved. And it is always directed toward a purpose. James states that purpose well when he says:

> Consider it pure joy, my brothers, whenever you face trials of many kinds, because you know that the testing of your faith develops perseverance. Perseverance must finish its work so that you may be mature and complete, not lacking anything.
>
> James 1:2–4

It is in waiting, both actively and passively, that maturity comes in our life. It is that maturity that brings completeness. It is that completeness that equips us to handle everything that may come our way. This indeed is what was happening in the life of Joseph. Scripture gives no indication of Joseph's complaining or murmuring. Though it seemed that he had been forgotten, he was quiet. Though things weren't on his timetable, he was patient. Though at times circumstances probably seemed unbearable, he was unwilling to surrender and collapse under them.

Wait Realistically

When waiting, one of the hardest things to remember is that God is never in a hurry. Though we work on a limited timetable, God works from and toward eternity. When God is in the process of making His man or woman, He will take the time needed to make that person the best he or she can be.

If you find yourself in a period of waiting, you must determine what it is you actually desire to be. Remember, to grow an oak takes a hundred years. On the other hand, to grow a flower requires only a few months. The difference is that the one stands the test of time and the other, though beautiful for a brief period, withers and dies. So it is with the spiritual realm. If you are to develop a character and life that will endure, you must be willing to allow God to take the time realistically needed to accomplish that end. Nothing that lasts happens quickly.

Paul said it eloquently in the New Testament: "Being confident of this, that he who began a good work in you will carry it on to completion . . ." (Philippians 1:6). It seems that Joseph had that kind of realism. He knew that the God who had brought him through every experience to date would complete the work that would make Joseph everything he was created with the potential of becoming. Somehow Joseph was able to grasp that God cannot be hurried.

Wait Cautiously

One final word about waiting. When the delay lengthens and an end is not in sight, the natural instinct is to begin to complain. It is too easy to begin to question such things as: Where is God? Doesn't He have my best interest at heart? Doesn't He know time is passing rapidly? All the good opportunities are passing me by!

It is here that a great danger arises. We begin to strive with sovereignty. Israel had that same problem. When in the Babylonian captivity, they waited for God to send a deliverer. They were convinced that He would be a strong Jewish firebrand. He would ride a white stallion and lead the Jews to victory over the Babylonian domination. Yet that is not how God chose to work. Years of captivity passed. Finally God raised up the one who would be the deliverer (literally "the messiah"). He was Cyrus, a gentile king. He was not even a believer in God; yet, he became His chosen instrument. Can you imagine the consternation of the Jews!

In Isaiah, chapter 45, God brings a word of caution to the Jews of that day and to us now. Repeatedly He says, "I am the Lord, and there is no other." Uncategorically He states His right to work out His sovereign plan in the lives of His people. It is in that context that He states, "Woe to him who quarrels with his Maker. . . . Does the clay say to the potter, 'What are you making?' " (v. 9.) God warns us about contesting His sovereignty.

There are two major ways we can test God's designed plan for our lives. On the one hand we may become totally passive in our relationship with Him. We do not give Him much attention. Our prayer life slacks off. We pray both weakly and weekly. Our time spent in His Word becomes minimal. We read for mileage more than content. When we do come across something relevant, we begin to think how it applies to everybody we know instead of us. Our desire to be with God's people also diminishes. We find it uncomfortable (due to conviction) to be with other believers. We don't want anything to remind us of our strained relationship with the Father.

On the other hand, we may involve ourselves in active rebellion. Our anger rises to the surface. Spiritually we shake our fist in God's face. We become angry at His action, or more often than not, His seeming inaction. Why isn't God on our time schedule? If He were only moving by our plan, things would be better.

Sometimes it is easy for us to have in mind a plan as to how we think God should deliver us from our waiting rooms. We desire the answer to be dramatic, as did the Jews. We have not only the method but, quite often, the timetable. And yet God will often not work according to either. Be careful lest you find yourself striving with God in the midst of these circumstances.

I have noticed some interesting tendencies about us as we wait in life. Three of them seem to surface repeatedly:

1. *We tend to look to God as a last resort rather than a first source.* Perhaps it is self-confidence. Perhaps it is pride. Maybe it is just stubbornness. Whatever the cause, too often we tend to bring God into our dilemmas too late. We strike out on our own, feeling that we are equal to anything. Sometimes you and I lapse into a "between a rock and a hard place" faith. We turn to God only when there seems to be no way out.

We need to learn to approach the Father on the front end. He knows of our every need before we even breathe it, so why do we keep it from Him so long? How much pain and wasted time could be saved if we just went to Him seeking His Word and counsel when the challenges begin!

2. *We desire deliverance by our timetable and method rather than His.* Be careful that you are not getting into the savior business. One of our biggest faults is that we become our own god. We assume that we know best how to handle the various circumstances that we face. It is easy in the self-sufficiency of our age to launch out on our own with a premeditated direction and agenda.

This was never the way God worked throughout Scripture. When He delivered His people, it was always in His time and His way. Whenever He lifted them to a new horizon of living, it was always done according to His road map. Be careful lest you, like the strong-willed child, are saying, "Please, I'd rather do it myself!"

3. *We border on preferring not to have an answer if God's answer doesn't agree with ours.* This was the position of the Jews with Cyrus. They would almost rather not have had God work on their behalf if He wasn't going to use a Jew. They had everything worked out in their minds and therefore had great difficulty accepting God's method of deliverance.

It's dangerous when you and I would rather have our way than to regroup and follow God's direction. It is in such stubbornness that we find His hand of discipline. God, like a parent, will lovingly do what He must to direct our lives as He determines best.

Even when He moves in our behalf, we sometimes complain as to His methodology. We question why He didn't do it our way. Our thought processes challenge His dealings in our life. Scripture pulls no punches when it warns us about striving with our Maker. Do you find yourself tempted to be in that position even now? Perhaps you need to reconsider your stance. Be careful, lest you miss the hand of God in the midst of your striving.

Perhaps you find yourself striving with God's sovereignty even now. If so, what can you do? First of all, get back to the basics. When Vince Lombardi, the successful coach of the Green Bay Packers, was seeing his team struggle, he faced the issue up front. He indicated that any group of naturally talented athletes could win more games than they lost. The key was concentrating on the fundamentals.

Following a close game lost by the Packers, Lombardi called a special Monday meeting. Standing before the players, he declared, "Men, we need to review the fundamentals of the game." Holding a football above his head, he continued, "This is a football." When we tend to buck God's hand on our life, we also must return to the fundamentals. This is the very time we need to be in His Word regularly. Yet, ironically enough, this is the very time we have little desire to be there. Though we don't feel much like praying, this is the very time that our communication with the Father must be clear and concise.

To get into God's Word, employ aids that will make it as enjoyable and interesting as possible. Such tools as Chuck Swindoll's *Come Before Winter* and *Growing Strong in the Seasons of Life* can make God's Word both relevant and alive when you are walking through difficult times. Such publishers as the Navigators and Campus Crusade have some very meaningful studies which you can use to help get back on the right track.

As to your prayer life, the best advice that I can give is to be honest. When we are striving with God, we often attempt to cover up. We pray—when we pray—as though nothing were really wrong. Do we fail to remember that God looks on the heart and doesn't just listen to the lips?

One of the most liberating things I've ever found in my Christian walk is the need and privilege of being honest with God. If you are struggling with His hand in your life right now, why don't you admit it to Him? Perhaps you might pray something like this:

Heavenly Father, right now I'm not happy with the way things are. I am frustrated with circumstances. Sometimes it seems as though You are a million miles away. Today I'm not sure that I love You or myself. I don't even feel a desire to be with other Christians. My hunger for Your Word is all but nonexistent. And honestly, I'm angry.

But Lord, I know this is not the way I should be. I admit that it is wrong. I ask You to change these attitudes in me. Restore to me the joy of my salvation. Create in my heart a hunger for Your Word, Your people, and You, Yourself. By faith, I thank You that You are already working in my heart to bring about these changes.

Be ready. Having asked in faith, things will change. Be sure your attitude is ready to let the changes take effect. You'll be glad you did!

A Time to Wait and a Time to Act

We have looked at some helpful guidelines on how to deal with life's waiting rooms. We must remind ourselves that always in the midst of waiting we are never without hope. The most profane word in our vocabulary should be the word *hopeless*. As you may be waiting for something right now, remember that nothing is impossible with God. When I find myself waiting, I am always reminded of the motto of the U.S. Army Corps of Engineers: "The difficult we do immediately; the impossible takes a little longer." I'm not sure about the army engineers but I know I've seen God do that over and over again. Though you may be disappointed as you stand in your time of waiting, remember that God can change your disappointments into His appointments.

When we've passed through a time of waiting, we must be careful that we are not lulled into inactivity and insensitivity. As important as it is to wait appropriately, it is just as important not to be always waiting for "something." Many people are wasting a lot of their lives sitting around waiting when God would have them actively stepping out in faith.

Psychologist William Moulton Marston conducted research using some three thousand people. He asked, "What have you to live for?" He was shocked when the findings indicated that 94 percent were simply enduring the present while they waited for the future. Some waited for "something to happen." Others waited for children to grow up and leave home. Others waited for next year, a long-dreamed-of trip, or for someone under their care to die. Regardless, it seemed that many were waiting for an elusive "tomorrow" without realizing the importance of today. There comes a time when we must be sure we are not living in yesterday, for it is gone—nor in tomorrow, for it may never come. In reality, we find ourselves living "in the meantime." We must honestly evaluate where we are in the present. If God has you in a time of waiting, be sure to wait effectively. But if the time of waiting is drawing to a conclusion, be sure you are not numbed into inactivity. Be willing to step out in the boldness of faith. Remember, life's waiting rooms not only have entrance doors, but exit doors as well.

POINTS TO PONDER

THE WAITING ROOMS OF LIFE

1. Why do you think we find waiting such a difficult part of life?
2. Why can waiting be a "top dollar" experience for our lives?
3. What does it mean to place your hope in God and His Word as you wait? How do you effectively accomplish that?
4. What can be learned about waiting by studying the history of the people of Israel?
5. What does it mean to strive with God's sovereignty? How do we do that?
6. After reading and thinking about waiting, if you had to counsel someone who was dealing with waiting, what would you say?

7

Witness While You Work

Snow White is one of my favorite movies. The cast is outstanding: Dopey, Doc, Sneezy, Bashful, Happy, Sleepy—and of course, my favorite, Grumpy. What a crew. I never could understand why they didn't win an Oscar for best supporting dwarfs.

Can't you still picture them in your mind? Marching through the lush forest glade, they challenged us to "Whistle While You

Work." It sounded so easy. And they made it look like so much fun. Maybe if you and I had a full orchestra backing us as we went off to work, we would have a lot more fun too.

"One thing is obvious," you are saying, "they didn't have the kind of job I have. If they did, they sure wouldn't be whistling! They would be sizzling!"

Okay, I will admit it. Work isn't always a nine-to-five cruise with the wind at your back and background music pounding out "O Happy Day." But one thing bothers me when I listen to so many Christians discuss what butters their bread. It seems more often than not the comments are negative. Something is wrong with the working environment. The boss isn't understanding. Colleagues are ruthless in their ambition. Their talent and brilliance are being overlooked.

While we may not whistle the day away at work, there is one thing we inevitably do—we witness. Have you stopped to check what type of witness you are giving where you work? It doesn't matter whether you work at home, in the professional community, in the vocational trades, or do volunteer work. What are you saying by how you are acting, talking, and performing?

The Making of a Model

Let's review Joseph's life and attempt to get a handle on witnessing while we work. One of the first things that jumps from the pages of Scripture is that Joseph didn't run throughout his respective jobs acting like a religious zealot. There is a common misconception that to witness at work one has to run around passing out tracts or cornering everyone, asking about the eternal condition of their souls. Personally I have seen more people turned off through that approach than I have seen turned on.

In order to witness while we work we must first remember what a witness is. A witness is one who gives evidence based on personal knowledge. This does not require that the witness be communicated in any particular format. In fact, the approach will vary from one person to another. Much will depend on temperament and personality. Your method may be quite different from my approach. We may both be different from Joseph. One thing is definite, however. We will each be a witness—either a good one or a poor one.

Allow me one additional comment before we return to Joseph. Many of us rationalize that we will witness by our lives. That sure sounds good and religious, doesn't it? There is only one problem. By itself it is inadequate. Regardless of how well we feel we may communicate via our life-style, we often leave confused spectators in our wake. They have no idea what makes the difference in our lives. They never will until we express it verbally. Life without lip leads to an incomplete witness.

Joseph combined the two well. His life portrayed that there was a different dynamic empowering him. Unhesitatingly he took advantage of every opportunity to verbally acknowledge the source of that driving force.

Now the question arises, how can you and I do the same?

A Character That Speaks

Have you ever noticed in life that there seem to be many characters but not many who have character. I'm not talking about reputation. Reputation is what we appear to be on the outside. Character is what we are on the inside. Character is the tempered steel which forms the superstructure of solid reputation.

Joseph exhibited a character that spoke volumes. Have you ever wondered what the key attributes were? Let's look at a few.

Loyalty. This is a difficult trait to find these days. Many simply flow with the wave of opinion and popularity. Others stumble over loyalty when potential conflict arises. Avoiding confrontation by nature, they jettison loyalty in order to avoid the possible discomfort of loyally standing strong to a person or issue.

Opportunity availed itself more than once for Joseph to choose comfort over loyalty. At the attempted seduction by Potiphar's wife, listen to Joseph's response:

> With me in charge, my master does not concern himself with anything in the house; everything he owns he has entrusted to my care. No one is greater in this house than I am. My master has withheld nothing from me except you, because you are his wife. How then could I do such a wicked thing and sin against God?
>
> Genesis 39:8–10

For Joseph, loyalty was of the utmost importance. To be disloyal to his boss would have been to sin against God. That was not due merely to the moral issue of a potentially illicit affair, though that would definitely have been sin. God also expects us to be loyal to those with whom we live.

Perhaps your temptation to be disloyal doesn't come in the person of the boss's wife. Perhaps instead it is your tongue. Do you find yourself criticizing your superior or colleagues? How about making them the brunt of poor humor or jokes? After you have agreed to a decision in private, do you back down in your support publicly when the heat begins to rise? When your job requires confidentiality, do you share those things which would best be kept private? Do you find it easy to rationalize by claiming that you are only "sharing your opinion"?

In enlisting leadership at our church we use a leadership covenant. It begins by enumerating qualities we desire in our leaders. The first of these is loyalty. One of the lines from this covenant says, "I promise I will not talk about you until I talk to you, and then I will only talk for you and never against you."

How are you measuring up to the plumb line Joseph established?

Noncritical spirit. Have you ever noticed that the easiest thing for some people to find is a problem or mistake? Especially if it is someone else's. It has never ceased to amaze me that Joseph never complained or criticized, even when he would have been so justified. Were you amazed that he did not testify to the true character of Potiphar's wife? Obviously Potiphar himself was uncertain in this regard, or Joseph would have been executed for such a charge.

Even in jail there is no record of critical attitude from Joseph. Undoubtedly he could have presented an outstanding "20/20" news special concerning the injustices of the system. Potiphar, the Pharaoh, and the warden could have been his prime targets on prime time. But not this man. He modeled a temperament under control.

Teddy Roosevelt summed it up when he said:

It is not the critic who counts; not the man who points out how the strong man stumbled, or where the doer of deeds could have done better. The credit belongs to the man who is actually in the arena; whose face is marred by dust and sweat and blood; who strives valiantly; who errs and comes short again and again because there is no effort without error and shortcoming; who does actually strive to do the deeds; who knows the great enthusiasm, the great devotions, spends himself in a worthy cause; who at the best knows in the end the triumph of high achievement; and who at the worst, if he fails at least fails while daring greatly, so that his place shall never be with those cold and timid souls who know neither victory nor defeat.[1]

That's my kind of man. That's Joseph. And it can be you and me.

By the way, do you know one of the best places to test your "critical attitude quotient"? It is your attitude about your supervisor. Some of us seem to have "boss criticitis." It seems at times that regardless of where some people work, or for whom, the boss is always a problem. Often this is characteristic of an authority problem. We just simply do not want any authority over us.

We must remind ourselves that everyone answers to some authority. It is inescapable whether it be government, a boss, church, or the family. God's Word instructs us to "do everything without complaining or arguing, so that you may become blameless and pure, children of God without fault in a crooked and depraved generation, in which you shine like stars in the universe" (Philippians 2:14, 15).

What is your attitude toward your boss? Concerning authority the Scripture counsels, "Obey your earthly masters with respect . . . and with sincerity of heart, just as you would obey Christ. Obey them not only to win their favor when their eye is on you. . . . Serve wholeheartedly, as if you were serving the Lord, not men, because you know that the Lord will reward everyone for whatever good he does . . ." (Ephesians 6:5–8). In order to witness while you work, make sure your "authority quotient" is in order.

Integrity. What Joseph was when alone in his private moments, he was in his open public ones. What you saw was what you got.

Somewhere I picked up a card entitled "A Busy Man's Creed." It says a lot about integrity.

> I believe in the stuff I am handing out, in the firm I am working for; and in my ability to get results. I believe that honest stuff can be passed out to honest men by honest methods. I believe in working, not weeping; in boosting, not knocking; and in the pleasure of my job. I believe that a man gets what he goes after, that one deed done today is worth two deeds tomorrow, and that no man is down and out until he has lost faith in himself. I believe in today and the work I am doing, in tomorrow and the work I hope to do, and in the sure reward which the future holds.

Add to that the underlying precept of faith in God's providence, and I suggest that our man Joe could have written that!

In biblical times potters were craftsmen. Their wares were displayed at every corner. The skilled hands of the more gifted artisans could produce works equal to today's fine china. These were said to be *sine cerus* (Latin), or "without wax." This meant there was no defect to be found.

Occasionally a bad apple would appear among the craftsmen. Rather than destroy a bad piece he would cover the defect with wax and then paint over it. The wise buyer would always hold the pottery up to the light. If it was defective, the waxed areas would appear much darker.

The Light still does that today. God reveals the cracks. We have two choices:

1. To see our cracks, acknowledge them, and allow the hand of the Master Craftsman to correct them.

2. Attempt to cover them or ignore them.

I was recently told of a financial company whose chief executive officer was retiring. A new man had to be chosen. The directors met and determined to promote within the company. Three vice-presidents were interviewed. The directors voted in a closed meeting to determine which of the candidates would become the new C.E.O.

A dynamic young man was selected. It was agreed that he would be brought in after lunch and the announcement would be made. With the major decision accomplished, the board recessed for lunch.

One of the board members went downstairs to the in-house snack bar to capture a few quiet moments along with a quick bite. The newly chosen young leader happened to be in line two people ahead of him. Busy about his business, the young man did not notice the board member behind him. As they moved through the line toward the register, the director saw the young man take some pats of butter. To the older gentleman's chagrin, he saw the newly elected president hide the pats under his napkin.

Returning to the directors' meeting the board member shared the unfortunate incident. Lively discussion ensued and action was taken. Finally the young man was summoned. Entering the boardroom, the youthful executive's excitement was obvious. He anticipated that he had been chosen to lead the institution into the future.

Within the glory of the moment the chairman's words reverberated through the room. "We had called you to announce that you had been chosen as the new leader of this company. Unfortunately, the scenario has changed. While at lunch you were observed taking some butter, hiding it, and not paying for it. One who leads this organization must have the highest integrity . . . even in the small things. Instead of promoting you, it is the decision of this board to ask for your immediate resignation."

The world is looking for a few good men—men of integrity!

Resiliency. One last quality exhibited by our star character is the ability to bounce back. Regardless of how difficult the circumstances, Joseph always overcame them. Rather than being under the pile, we always find him scaling the mountains of adversity. We seem to see so many who give up too quickly. Rather than stand their ground, they crumble in the face of difficulty. Thank goodness Stephen Hawking wasn't like that.

Stephen is the one who finally was able to explain Einstein's Unified Field Force. Einstein had tried for thirty years to show why light is distorted while traveling through gravitational fields in space. A clear explanation had eluded him. Hawking proposed that the reason was black holes. These were burned-out hulks of dead and collapsed stars.

At thirty-two years of age he presented his theory at Oxford. In doing so, his speech was unintelligible. He required assistance due to the fact that he could not stand or walk. Questions addressed to his presentation were answered by an interpreter. He could not write either. You see, Stephen suffered from "Lou Gehrig's disease."

Upon hearing his presentation, the professors realized they were watching brilliance in action. He was admitted to the university. The rest is history—including a Disney movie about the phenomenon.

How easy it is to quit. Anyone can do it. But no one who makes a difference does! An anonymous poet put it well:

I have taught a class for many years;
Bore many burdens—toiled through tears;
But folks don't notice me a bit,
I'm so discouraged—I'll just quit.

Some time ago I joined the choir
That many souls I might inspire;
But folks don't seem moved a bit
So what use to sing? I'll just quit.

I've labored long in women's work,
And not a task did ever shirk,
But folks have talked a little bit
And I won't stand it. I'll just quit.

I've led young people day and night
And sacrificed to lead them right,
But folks won't help me out a bit
And I'm so tired, I think I'll quit.

Christ's cause is hindered everywhere
And folks are dying in despair.
The reason why? Just a bit.
The church is full of folks who quit.

Anybody can do it. The choice is ours.

Actions Speak at Least as Loud as Words

Hand in hand with Joseph's character were his actions. Two active traits stand out to me above all others in Joseph's life—a servant attitude and excellence.

A servant attitude. Joseph seems to have continually looked for ways to do things for others. When we first met him, he was working in the family business. There he was, attempting to look out for the interests of his father. Next it was Potiphar. Following that came the warden in the prison. Even in prison he gave himself to helping the Pharaoh's cupbearer and baker. All of this was a training ground to enable him to serve all of Egypt, the most powerful country of that day.

The problem is that when we think of a servant, we usually picture a shy, gutless wonder who couldn't do anything other than be a doormat for others. The other mental picture is of someone who comes to our table and queries, "May I take your order or get you something to drink?"

We have lost the strength that inherently belongs with servanthood. It takes a much bigger person to serve than to be served. Joseph proved that. So did a Galilean carpenter by the name of Jesus. The Apostle Paul wasn't too bad at serving either, and what a strong personality he was! It was he who said, "Do nothing out of selfish ambition or vain conceit, but in humility consider others better than yourselves" (Philippians 2:3).

Paul goes on to paint an incredible picture of the Master Servant—Jesus Christ. It is the ultimate picture of strength. Being God in nature, Jesus willingly stepped from the splendor of heaven to take on a new role—that of a servant. That required Him to leave His comfort zone. All servanthood requires that the one serving leave his or her comfort zones. That includes you and me.

Serving by its very nature requires risk. No one has said it is easy. It is only in this mode that life has a cutting edge. If we are to live on the edge of adventure, serving others is where we will find it.

Someone has said there are three classes of people:

1. The risk takers
2. The caretakers
3. The undertakers

If you and I are not risking ourselves we have lapsed into a maintenance mode of living. It doesn't take long for that to lead to a regressing life-style where our main focus becomes ourselves and others are ignored. At that point we not only become undertakers but we take others under with us.

Perhaps the greatest risk in serving is the risk of becoming vulnerable. To become vulnerable is to risk being disappointed, hurt, or abused. Who would know that better than the Master Servant? All of those things happened to Him when He became vulnerable. But look at what He accomplished in that vulnerability!

Author Creath Davis summed our position up well when he said:

> . . . it really is risky to be vulnerable enough to care. Failing to care for others causes the soul to shrivel and may deprive another of help only we could give. Perhaps the most expensive area of personal exposure is in the risk of being known, not as a super-saint, but as a struggler.[2]

But I guarantee that if you are willing to risk that kind of openness, your life will come alive!

Lest you think this is only a biblical opinion, let me share with you from another perspective. In his outstanding book *A Passion for Excellence*, Tom Peters quoted a leading executive as saying, "The role of the leader is a servant's role. It's supporting his people, running interference for them. It's coming out with an atmosphere of understanding and trust—and love. . . . Tyranny is not allowed here."[3]

Along the same line Bim Black of Teleflex Corporation said of the servanthood approach:

- People are people . . . not personnel.

- People don't dislike work . . . help them understand mutual objectives, and they'll drive themselves to unbelievable excellence.

- The best way to really train people is with an experienced mentor . . . and on the job.

- People have ego and development needs . . . and they'll commit themselves only to the extent that they can see ways of satisfying these needs.

- People cannot be truly motivated by anyone else . . . that door is locked from the inside; they should work in an atmosphere that fosters self-motivation . . . self-assessment . . . and self-confidence.

- People should work in a climate that is challenging, invigorating, and fun . . . and the rewards should be related as directly as possible to performance.

- When people are in an atmosphere of trust, they'll put themselves at risk; only through risk is there growth . . . reward . . . self-confidence . . . leadership.[4]

In different ways it all says the same thing: *Give yourself away.* That's one gift that if we try to hold on to we will ultimately lose.

As I observe Joseph, I wonder why the older he became the more of a servant's heart he gained. Could it be that he learned something from his experience of relating his dreams of destiny to his family? No doubt the dreams were from the Lord. There are times when I wonder not so much about the subject of the dreams as the manner in which he told the dreams. Could it possibly have come across, due to his youth and enthusiasm, a bit on the self-serving side? We have no way of knowing for sure.

One thing is certain. The reaction of his brothers was *strong*. Maybe over the years there had been a subtle lesson learned. Real strength comes in serving. Had the years mellowed Joseph? Oh, he had not backed down at all. He was still unafraid to take a strong stand. But there is a difference between being yellow and being mellow. Servanthood will have a gentle character to it, even in the context of a strong personality.

If you are looking to witness through your actions, look for someone at the office you can serve. Go out of your way to make your customer, or potential customer for that matter, feel that he or she is the most important person in the world to you. Find someone to whom you can pay a sincere compliment. Ask your boss if there is anything extra you can do just to help. But be ready. He might be struck speechless. Ask someone who works for you what you could do to help. If you do that, I'll guarantee he or she will faint. But you'll find it doesn't hurt. In fact, it feels good. Try it, you'll like it!

Excellence. Joseph was also characterized by this commendable trait in his every deed. If it was worth doing, it was worth doing right. And the results were amazing. He prospered in everything he did. Whether it was in the pits of prison or at the pinnacle of power made no difference to Joseph.

But how is excellence attained? Does it demand perfection in all we do? Hardly. If it did, you might as well quit reading now. But excellence does presuppose a standard. Otherwise how will we know if we reach it?

Our standard today is not unlike Joseph's. Paul set it forth well when he said, "And whatever you do, whether in word or deed, do it all in the name of the Lord Jesus, giving thanks to God the

Father through him" (Colossians 3:17). Granted, Jesus had not come in Joseph's time. But He existed. He has existed from time immemorial. And Joseph's standard was to do all he did so that it would be pleasing to God. When that's your standard, it's hard to produce sloppy work!

My good friend Leighton Ford serves as the chairman of the Lausanne Committee for World Evangelization. Recently he was discussing ministry strategies with lay leaders representing various organizations from around North America. One of the men represented a group of Christians employed by one of America's great corporations. This group has initiated numerous Bible studies which are open to all employees. Many have attended and a great number of those have become Christians. A great host of others have become more confident in their faith.

In elaborating on the ministry, this gentleman made an outstanding observation. He indicated, "We have determined that there is an even more important avenue of witnessing than through our Bible studies. That avenue is through displaying excellence in our work." What an insight!

I cringe when an employer tells me that he or she is not sure they want to hire anyone who claims to be a strong Christian because they have had too many disappointments with such people. Other times I have been told that some "Christian" has displayed one of the worst attitudes in the work place. Or they take advantage of a Christian boss and, as a result, loaf on the job. Still others bring their problems to work with them on a daily basis.

If we are to impact the marketplace, there must be a difference in our lives! If we are to be salt, we should live and work so as to make others thirsty for that which makes a difference in our lives. In order to be light we must illuminate the correct attitudes and work habits. The world cannot be allowed to squeeze us into its mold. Instead, we are called to reshape the world's mold. As the world wallows in mediocrity, you and I are challenged to a new standard—*excellence*.

By the way, remember it is excellence, not perfection. One you can live with, the other will enslave you.

A Strategy for Witnessing

I know, you're asking, "Where do I go from here?" Well, I would suggest a simple threefold strategy. It is nothing magical, but it is very practical.

Preparation. In anything we do, the better the preparation, the better the results. A runner spends hours straining and sweating to get into proper condition to run well. A swimmer spends so much time in the water, he comes near to getting waterlogged. Preparation is an essential element in life.

It is the same with witnessing. You must ready yourself for the task. That begins with learning a methodology by which you can effectively communicate your faith. Today there are many available. Evangelism Explosion offers a Gospel presentation that is to be learned and memorized. This then serves as tracks on which to run as you share your faith with someone. Eventually you learn to share your faith in Christ with anyone, anywhere, at any time. Campus Crusade and the Billy Graham Crusades also offer outstanding tools and training for witnessing.

Books are another invaluable resource for your preparation. I highly recommend *How to Give Away Your Faith* by Paul Little, *Life-Style Evangelism* by Joseph Aldrich, *How to Witness Successfully* by George Sweeting, and *Winning Ways* by Leroy Eims. In each of these you will find a treasury of helps for practical, powerful witnessing strategies. You will also fulfill the scriptural injunction to ". . . always be prepared to give an answer to everyone who asks you to give the reason for the hope that you have. But do this with gentleness and respect . . ." (1 Peter 3:15, 16).

One final word on preparation. You must also build relationships with those with whom you wish to share. That means you must build a bridge to them. It is interesting that the Latin word for *priest* means "bridge builder." Am I saying that you must do whatever it takes in order to gain an opportunity to witness, even if it means compromise? By no means!

What I am saying is that you need to find some common interest point and begin to build a relationship. When I was in business, I became friends with an engineer. We both enjoyed golf a great deal. Following a circumstance in which he had provided a very helpful service to me, I invited him to a round of golf. During the round, he began to talk about his religious background and to ask me a great deal about the Bible. We would hit the ball and talk, hit the ball and talk, hunt for the ball and talk.

When we finished, we were standing in the parking lot, and he asked how he could have a personal relationship with Christ like we had talked about. Briefly I shared the answer with him. I was able to do that because along the way I had prepared how to talk to others about the Christian faith. Within moments, right there in the parking lot, he was praying, asking Christ to enter his heart. What a way to end a golf game! Who cares about the score!

Prayer. You must pray primarily for two things: opportunities and boldness. I am convinced that none of us lacks for opportunities. Our real problem is that we do not recognize them when they come. We are so busy with our schedules and routines that we pass people like ships in the night. Opportunities escape us on a daily basis.

One of the people I have had the joy of seeing trained in how to give away his faith is my friend Tom. He became challenged on this very issue. His prayer became that God would make him aware of possibilities to witness when he happened on them. So far it must be working. Tommy has led to Christ his sister while watching a stock car race, a guard at one of the companies he calls on, a family he met at a restaurant . . . and that is only the tip of the iceberg. And Tommy is multiplied over and over in other friends such as Don Hoover, Robin Carter, Robert Brown, and so many more. These are people just like you—people who are praying to be aware of divine appointments that God gives them during their normal daily routines.

There is one other essential ingredient—boldness. That has nothing to do with your temperament, by the way. It is a divine enabling from the Lord. I have seen some of the most shy people become amazingly bold.

Paul thought it was important. He asked of the Ephesian Church, "Pray also for me, that whenever I open my mouth, words may be given me so that I will fearlessly make known the mystery of the gospel" (Ephesians 6:19). The church prayed for it throughout the Book of Acts. So should we.

Are you nervous about talking to others about Christ? Join the club! So am I at times. But God is faithful to give boldness if it is requested. And once it is prayed for, just like swimming, dive in when you get the chance.

Proclaim. Remember what we have discussed. You and I proclaim in many ways—by our character, our actions, and our words. In everything we do we are witnessing. The question is, what kind of witness are we being? A silent one? A two-faced one? An unclear one? A prepared and prayerful one? We make the choice.

One final thought. Be careful that you do not compromise your witness in one area with an errant action in another area. For instance, if you have the opportunity to talk with someone about the Christian faith, do it on your own time, not the company's. Don't become a pest so that people dart away and hide when they see you coming. Be careful about being all talk and no walk. In essence, be sure you are balanced in your witness. The results will amaze you.

Remember, whether you feel like whistling while you work or not, you will be a witness.

POINTS TO PONDER

WITNESS WHILE YOU WORK

1. How did Joseph witness while he worked? How do you?
2. Of the key attributes exhibited in Joseph's life, which are strongest in your life? Which do you have the greatest struggle with?
3. Why is it easier to have a critical spirit than a noncritical spirit toward authority?
4. Are there ways in which you could better express excellence in your work (home, school, business)?
5. Pick a day this week and covenant to do everything you can to serve others where you "work" without letting them know why or expecting anything in return.
6. Take a pen and paper and write down a plan for strengthening your witness where you "work."

8
The Indispensable Ingredient

> **MAXIM:**
>
> For successful Christian living, the key is not how much of the Holy Spirit you have, but how much of you the Holy Spirit has.

It's one of the fondest memories I have of growing up. I looked forward to the adventure with eager anticipation each time. It was always a journey into the enjoyable.

Mother would always make sure I looked as nice as possible. That meant even tucking my shirttail in! So much for the dirt behind my ears, too. And there was the cowlick. She would plaster it down until she thought it would remain in place. Then it would rise again, as though powered by a hydraulic lift. As you can tell, just getting ready for the adventure was an experience.

Then off we would go ... shopping. Our destination was downtown. And the first store we always stopped in was Sears Roebuck.

As we entered the store, my eyes began to bulge with expectancy. Could I get some popcorn? Or how about some candy? Would we see our friend who worked in the shoe department who always had some special surprise waiting for me? And if I was really lucky, maybe I could even weasel a toy out of Mom.

Perhaps the thing I remembered most is that every time we entered the store, I saw the law being broken. In the center of the main aisle was the vacuum cleaner display. In a way that I didn't understand then, they had reversed the airflow direction of the vacuum cleaner. Instead of sucking, it was blowing. The hose was propped just right to be able to suspend a beach ball in midair, held aloft by the airstream of the vacuum cleaner. The law being broken, of course, was the law of gravity. But it never ceased to amaze me how air could accomplish such an unusual feat.

As the years have passed, I have continued to be fascinated by the power of air. I learned that in the 1940s Westinghouse Airbrake Company had first made the controls to stop railroad cars—all with the use of air. Next came air controls for diesel engines on tugboats. By using airflow, the direction of the diesel engine could be changed. Air brakes for semitrucks were combined with air-powered shock absorbers to literally give a "ride on air."

In more recent days, air has surpassed our imagination in what it can accomplish. For instance, are you aware that most surgical tools in operating rooms are powered by air? Or how about the Firestone actuator? Have you used one of those recently? I doubt it. The actuator looks like a large inner tube without a hole in it. Deflated, it is placed under a railroad car. Add air and—*voilá!* The car can be lifted right off the ground. The Firestone actuator is used to lift railroad cars when they need to be turned.

Or how about what are now called multimotion actuators. They appear to be deflated gloves. But add air and they become robotic in nature. The fingers become flexible and are able to pick up and move items.

In considering air, think also of the power of air in nature. I have seen it deroot the strongest of trees. Drinking straws have been driven through telephone poles in the midst of a tornado. I've seen the aftermath of cars picked up by the wind and with crushing power, welded together.

Have you ever been at the beach as a hurricane is approaching? All right, I agree it is not the most practical place to be—but it's awesome. The wind drives the waves as they lash against the shore in fury. Palm trees begin to bend like ballerinas stretching at the bar.

Wind is a powerful force.

As we move through life, we tend to think in the realm of "out of sight, out of mind." And since you can't see air or the wind, often we don't give it much thought. It is much like that with the Spirit of God. Since we can't see it or handle it, we tend to put it on the back burner of our mind.

It is interesting to note that air and wind are used as the analogies of God's Spirit in the Bible. In the Old Testament the Hebrew word used is *ruach*. Its Greek equivalent is *pneuma*. Both indicate "wind, breath, or air." The Holy Spirit moves where and as He will—like the wind. But even though He is out of sight, He should never be out of mind.

We see this in Joseph's life. After he had been released from prison, he interpreted Pharaoh's dream. There would be seven years of abundance followed by seven years of famine. But the interpretation of the dream isn't where it ended.

Joseph went on to offer counsel to Pharaoh. He should look for a wise man to put in charge of the land of Egypt. They should begin to prepare for the seven years of abundance. This government farm bill would allow them to survive through the coming difficult times.

Pharaoh's response to Joseph's unsolicited advice is remarkable:

> The plan seemed good to Pharaoh and to all of his officials. So Pharaoh asked them, "Can we find anyone like this man, one in whom is the Spirit of God?" Then Pharaoh said to Joseph, "Since God has made all this known to you, there is no one so discerning and wise as you. You shall be in charge of my palace, and all my people are to submit to your orders. Only with respect to the throne will I be greater than you."
>
> Genesis 41:37–40

Did you notice the summation of Joseph? His wisdom stood forth prominently. But the reason for the wisdom was attributed to the Spirit of God. God's Spirit had made a difference in Joseph's life. Now Joseph was making a difference in the lives of many others.

To make a difference in your own life, and the lives of those around you, the Holy Spirit is indispensable.

A Case of Mistaken Identity

Unfortunately, when the Holy Spirit is discussed, many get the wrong perception. Their understanding is cloudy at best. Things and characteristics which have nothing to do with the Holy Spirit are credited to His account. Other key attributes go totally unrecognized or ignored.

Allow me, if I may, to dispel a few of the misconceptions about this key member of the Trinity:

The Holy Spirit is not an impersonal "it." The Bible refers to the Holy Spirit as a person, not an "it." He is animate and not inanimate. The Bible gives Him numerous personal characteristics:

1. **Kindness**   (Nehemiah 9:20).

2. **A will**   (1 Corinthians 12:11).

3. **Love**   (Romans 15:30).

4. **The ability to comfort**   (John 14).

5. **A mind**   (Romans 8:27).

With qualities such as these, the Spirit cannot possibly be an it. Instead, He is active, alive, and personable. He is capable of both knowing and being known.

The Holy Spirit is not a Casper, the Friendly Ghost. Due to the fact that the Bible occasionally designates the Holy Spirit as the Holy Ghost, many have developed interesting mental pictures. You remember Casper, the Friendly Ghost. He was always there doing good and helping those in need. He was rather shy and introverted. His desire was to be good, well liked, and useful.

For many that depicts the Holy Spirit—an invisible secret agent who is able to act on our behalf as any good ghost should. He is there to help us when we are in a bind and need some behind-the-scenes help—an apparition to be called upon to do our bidding. Scripture nowhere gives this account of God's Spirit. As we deal with a Holy God, we must be careful to avoid cartoon characterizations of the active agent of His personality in today's world.

A mother recently told me about her son, who was busily drawing a work of art. When she asked what he was drawing, he responded, "The Holy Spirit." "But nobody knows what the Holy Spirit looks like," his mother responded. "They will when I get through!" the budding theologue replied. Though all of us may have our own concept of the Holy Spirit, we must remember that He is the Holy God. He cannot be reduced to an image on paper.

The Holy Spirit is not a "warm, fuzzy feeling." Since the beginning of man's religious quest, he has looked for the "warm fuzzies" of religion. Experiences that are emotional. Ecstatic and euphoric states. Effervescent emotions.

Feelings have often offset faith. Whereas God says faith is the key criterion in a relationship with Him, man has tried to replace it with faulty feelings. Rather than taking God at His Word, man wants to live by his own emotions. But how can that work when man's emotions and feelings are affected by what he eats? How much sleep he gets or doesn't get? Circumstances? And on and on it goes.

Joseph's Hidden Helper

Pharaoh recognized a dimension in Joseph's life not found in the lives of his counselors, magicians, and servants. It wasn't as though Joseph had tried to hide this inner source. When asked if he could interpret Pharaoh's dream, he readily replied, "I cannot do it, but God will give Pharaoh the answer he desires" (Genesis 41:16). God had been active in Joseph's life for some years. Now the most preeminent leader of all the world recognized the ramifications. Though he did not understand Joseph's God, Pharaoh saw the power of God's Spirit upon Joseph's life.

Throughout the Old Testament, God put His Holy Spirit on several of His people. Each time, the Holy Spirit empowered that person to perform special God-ordained tasks. His Spirit was put on Gideon to lead Israel in a crucial time in its history (Judges 6:34). David was anointed with God's Spirit to be the king of God's people (1 Samuel 16:13). Moses was anointed to be a wise leader of God's people in their exodus from Egypt (Numbers 11:25).

But just as the Holy Spirit could be placed on a person in the Old Testament, it was also removed at times. King Saul had the Spirit removed when he was disobedient to God's commands (1 Samuel 16:14). Samson became so disobedient and insensitive to God's direction for his life that he was not even aware when God's Spirit left him (Judges 16:20). David, in great remorse for his sin with Bathsheba, prayed that God would not allow His Spirit to depart from him (Psalms 51:11).

The Holy Spirit is also spoken as being "in" some Old Testament characters. Numbers 27:18 refers to the Holy Spirit as being in Joshua. This is how Pharaoh also described God's Spirit in relation to Joseph. This most probably describes the special touch of God upon the lives of these men. It was not until the New Testament, however, that the Holy Spirit came to permanently indwell God's people. The Old Testament only saw it happen as an anointing from God for special service.

Regardless of where God's Spirit is mentioned as touching the lives of Old Testament leaders, there is always one condition that made it possible—*obedience*.

The Spirit of Our Age

Since the days of Joseph, the Holy Spirit has not changed. But His function and role have. Whereas in the Old Testament, He was involved in creation, followed by the anointing of God-chosen people for God-chosen tasks, today His role is different. But before we get into that, let's quickly look at just who the Holy Spirit really is.

The Holy Spirit is the Holy God. He is not merely a messenger of God, the Father. Nor is He a mere expression of God. Still further, He is not merely a manner of speech referring to the God of the Bible. Instead, He *is* God! The Bible refers to Him and gives Him divinity at several points:

1. The Spirit of the Father   (Matthew 10:20).

2. The Spirit of the Lord God   (Isaiah 61:1).

3. The Spirit of the Lord   (Isaiah 11:2).

4. The Spirit of our God   (1 Corinthians 6:11).

5. The Holy Spirit and God are one and the same
(Acts 5:3, 4).

In addition, the Holy Spirit is given divine attributes. Just a few of these are:

1. Omniscience   (1 Corinthians 2:10, 11).

2. Omnipresence   (Psalms 139:7).

3. Omnipotence   (Zechariah 4:6).

But not only is the Holy Spirit the person of God, He is also the gift from God. "Do you not know that your body is a temple of the Holy Spirit, who is in you, whom you have received from God? . . ." (1 Corinthians 6:19). In our day, the New Testament era, God gives His Holy Spirit as a gift to those who believe.

Most probably your first question is, "When is that gift given?" It happens at the time one transfers his trust to Christ alone for his eternal salvation. Therefore, it is given the moment one places his belief in Jesus Christ as Lord and Savior.

With these two foundational truths in mind, let's look together at what the Holy Spirit does. As we walk through these things, I must remind you that here I cannot give a thorough study of the Holy Spirit. I would encourage you to do that on your own, as you will find it a most rewarding venture. Let's look together in an overview of what the Spirit of God accomplishes within our lives.

142

As we look at these, there will be no doubt left as to why the Spirit of God is the indispensable ingredient for successful Christian living.

The Holy Spirit convicts. The Bible tells us that it is the Spirit of God that shows us our need for a personal relationship with Jesus Christ.

> When he comes, he will convict the world of guilt in regard to sin and righteousness and judgment: in regard to sin, because men do not believe in me; in regard to righteousness, because I am going to the Father, where you can see me no longer; and in regard to judgment, because the prince of this world now stands condemned.
>
> John 16:8–11

In convicting us of our need for a relationship with God, the Holy Spirit first convicts us of sin within our life. This is different from convicting us of sins (acts, attitudes, thoughts, and so on). Sin referred to here is the sinful nature with which we are born. It is revealed in the tendency to do things our own way rather than God's way. We stand condemned before God because of our sinful nature. As awareness comes concerning the need for a change within our life, we are led to understand that we do not need an internal evolution but a revolution.

The Spirit also convicts us as He shows us the pure righteousness of Jesus Christ. In seeing God for who He really is, we see ourselves for who we really are. This is why in Luke 5, after seeing Jesus perform such a miracle, Peter fell to his knees and said, "Go away from me, Lord; I am a sinful man!" (v. 8). It is the same reason that in Isaiah 6 the prophet, having personally realized the greatness of God, said, "Woe to me! I am ruined! For I am a man of unclean lips . . . and my eyes have seen the King, the Lord Almighty" (v. 5). As the Spirit reveals God's perfectness, our sinfulness becomes even more evident.

Nowhere is our sin more evident than in our relaxing the standards for right and wrong. We don't even like to use the word *wrong* anymore. To many ears, it sounds prehistoric and archaic. As a result, we have established justifications for what used to be a clear demarcation between black and white. Unfortunately, between those two poles, we have developed a large area of gray. Writer Meg Greenfield offers some of the alternatives that we have substituted for right and wrong.

> RIGHT AND STUPID: . . . Wrong is dumb, breathtakingly dumb, and therefore unfathomable; so, conveniently the effort to fathom it may just as well be called off. . . .
>
> RIGHT AND NOT NECESSARILY UNCONSTITU-TIONAL: This is the avoidance of admitting that something is wrong by pointing out that it is not specifically or even inferentially prohibited by the Constitution or the Criminal Code or The Ten Commandments. . . .
>
> RIGHT AND SICK: Crime or lesser wrongdoing defined as physical or psychological disorder—this one has been around for ages. . . .
>
> RIGHT AND ONLY TO BE EXPECTED: This is probably the most popular dodge, used to justify every kind of lapse. . . .[1]

As these arguments proliferate today, absolutes become more and more muddled. Though society attempts to explain it away, God's Spirit remains constant. To Him, sin is sin. He continues to use our conscience and the Word of God to show us that absolutes are still as solid today as the very day they were created.

But the Holy Spirit does not stop there. He goes on to show that there is hope. He states that God has executed judgment on the one who wishes to exploit our sinful nature—Satan, himself. The final conflict was staged at Calvary. Satan's doom was sealed. With eternal vision, Jesus Himself had predicted it when He exclaimed, "I saw Satan fall like lightning from heaven" (Luke 10:18). With that prophetic utterance, history took a new turn.

The Holy Spirit makes God relevant. When conviction has occurred, the Spirit of God then moves to show us the relevancy of God in our lives. As you and I make the decision to ask Christ into our lives, the Holy Spirit makes our spiritual nature come alive in our hearts. His Word is made relevant to our daily living and everyday decisions. Through all of this, the Holy Spirit is communicating God's mind to us (John 16:14).

In a day in which so much is seen as irrelevant, our hearts cry for a relevant God. Many try to cope with our challenging times in different ways. Some turn to alcohol, others to drugs—escape mechanisms.

Curtis Wright was a bit more creative. He would not have impressed you had you met him. He was a normal, hail-fellow-well-met, ordinary, run-of-the-mill, guy next door. He was also a grouch. And like many of us, he hated Mondays. He did a great deal of research to prove that Mondays were, indeed, disasters. He found that Mondays had held a number of rather dismal events:

Napoleon invaded Russia.

The Titanic sank.

Rudolph Valentino died.

First-class postage was increased by fifteen cents.

Senate Watergate hearings opened.

Not one to let a challenge go untackled, Wright decided to do something about it. He created a calendar with no Mondays on it.

It had Sunday, Tuesday, Wednesday, Thursday, Friday, and Saturday. But Mondays just disappeared. All that was left was a gaping hole between Sunday and Tuesday.

Though that's the kind of calendar you may feel you need, it's not the answer. Instead of trying to do away with Mondays, you and I need to find the God who is so relevant that He enables us to handle our "Mondays" of life. It is only by the Holy Spirit that we will find the God who is equal to the task.

The Holy Spirit takes up residence in our hearts. Upon a decision to transfer our trust to Christ for eternal salvation, God moves in. He comes in the person of the Holy Spirit. Whereas in the Old Testament, the Holy Spirit would come upon men for special tasks and even fill them temporarily, He now comes to stay eternally. "Don't you know that you yourselves are God's temple and that God's Spirit lives in you?" (1 Corinthians 3:16).

The moment we become Christians, a new tenant occupies the rooms of our life, desiring access into every area of our daily living. And once He is there, He has claimed rights eternally. He is not a temporary tenant but a long-term resident. Until life ends, His home will be our hearts.

The Holy Spirit establishes ownership. The Bible refers to it as the Holy Spirit "sealing" us (Ephesians 1:13; 4:30). This act establishes God's ownership upon our lives. Paul used this term primarily as he was writing to the Ephesian Church. Since that was a commercial trade center, the use of the seal was common in daily life. This was especially true in the timber trades. When timber was selected in Ephesus, the buyer would affix his seal to his purchase. This would protect the timber until it could be transported to its final destination. In the same way, the Holy Spirit shows God's ownership on our lives until we are transported to our final destination—eternity with God, the Father. That is why Paul told Timothy that as a result of our being sealed, the ". . . Lord knows those who are his . . ." (2 Timothy 2:19).

The Holy Spirit is a down payment of our inheritance. When God moves into our lives, He puts a down payment on the future. That payment is in the person of the Holy Spirit. He serves as the "holding agent" or earnest payment for what God has in store for us.

Again, in writing to the Ephesian Church, Paul indicates that the Holy Spirit is a "deposit guaranteeing our inheritance until the redemption of those who are God's possession . . ." (Ephesians 1:14). This also is a commercial term. It was used in biblical days in selling land. After the seller had accepted a down payment, he could not change his mind and refuse to fulfill the contract terms. The purchaser, as well, was obligated to the terms. Following the receipt of the initial down payment, the seller would often give the purchaser a handful of soil. This marked a sample of what the buyer would acquire upon full payment.

God has made full payment for our inheritance in eternity. That payment was Jesus Christ and the cross. But until the time we join Him in heaven, the Holy Spirit serves as the down payment or earnest payment of what lies before us. He is God's guarantee!

The Holy Spirit places us in Christ. The biblical term is that we are "baptized" in Christ. This pictures one being immersed in the Savior. It is just another way of saying that our entire environment and spirit of living become Christ-centered.

In addition, we are placed in Christ so that when God looks at us, following conversion, He sees not us, but Christ. To be baptized by the Holy Spirit into the body of Christ is a one-time event. Scripturally, this is described in Acts 1:5, Romans 6:3, and 1 Corinthians 12:13. It is this baptism which brings us into vital union with Jesus Christ and allows for no distinction among believers in this respect. It is in this way that the Holy Spirit adds to the church.

The Holy Spirit anoints us. This anointing is referred to in 2 Corinthians 1:21, 22. Anointing in the days of biblical writers was set aside for two groups—kings and priests. This official act symbolically gave them authority and power to carry out their responsibilities. In the same way the anointing of the Holy Spirit gives the believer the full authority of God.

The Scripture uses a word for "authority" which is *exousia*. It stands for authority which is delegated. In Matthew 28:18, Jesus declared that God, the Father, had given "all authority" in heaven and earth. Luke 10:19 finds Him, in turn, giving that authority to His disciples. This delegated power is always backed by the power in whose name it is given. Even today when one acts in the authority of another, he acts in the full authority of the one he represents. That is the position of an ambassador. When he speaks, he speaks for his nation. That is why the Scripture says that you and I are ambassadors for Christ (2 Corinthians 5:20).

The Holy Spirit also infuses us with power to live life successfully. You and I are referred to as kings in Revelation 1:5 and priests in 1 Peter 2:9. As a result of that standing before God, we are given power as recorded in Acts 1:8 to live life in a dynamic fullness of God's presence.

In Scripture the word *dunamis* is used for power. It is the same word from which we get "dynamite," "dynamic," and "dynamo." It represents an explosive, charging power. It only happens as the Holy Spirit is able to fully control and direct our lives.

One of the finest descriptions I've ever come across was stated by J. B. Phillips. In his introduction to *Letters to Young Churches*, he says:

The great difference between present-day Christianity and that of which we read in these letters [New Testament Epistles] is that to us it is primarily a performance, to them it was a real experience. We are apt to reduce the Christian religion to a code, or at best a rule of heart and life. To these men it is quite plainly the invasion of their lives by a new quality of life altogether. They do not hesitate to describe this as Christ "living in" them.

The Holy Spirit gives us security. In this world in which we strive to be secure, God grants it as a gift. In daily living, the way that you and I attain security within ourselves is by others' telling us of their love, encouragement, and belief in our worth. It is through such assurance that self-esteem and security are solidified as you and I grow.

God does the same thing through the Holy Spirit. "The Spirit himself testifies with our spirit that we are God's children" (Romans 8:16). As the Spirit of God testifies with our inner spirit, He affirms our worth in God's sight. He enlivens God's Word as we read it. He mediates our prayers to our Heavenly Father. He communicates God's love and encouragement to us in the inner sensitivity of our private world.

The Holy Spirit enables us. Once you and I are in a right relationship with Jesus Christ, His Son, the Holy Spirit prepares us to minister to others. This preparation is accomplished through spiritual gifts. This equips us as members of God's church for two things: (1) effective ministry and (2) inevitable conflict with the powers of darkness. These gifts are referred to as *charismata* or gifts of grace. They have nothing to do with our merit or deserving them. They are always given for ministry to others rather than to be cherished or haughtily displayed. For the most part they are gifts of service of some type.

Everyone receives at least one gift. As Christians we must learn to appropriate our gifts. This comes only by experience, through the study of God's Word, and the affirmation of others. The gift will be eternal but its use will depend upon us. If not used, like muscles, the gifts will atrophy. How are you doing with yours?

Prepare to Make a Difference

I am sure that you, like me, have been amazed as you have focused on the attributes of God's Spirit. The things that He does for us are immeasurable in worth. These alone should make anyone want to be in proper relationship with God through Jesus Christ.

God provides one additional thing for us that was not available to Joseph. He offers the opportunity to be filled with His Holy Spirit. In fact, He commands it when He says, ". . . be filled with the Spirit" (Ephesians 5:18). God desires to do it for us even more than we desire to have it. When Jesus said He would send "another Comforter," He referred to the Spirit of God. The word He used for *another* means "one of the same kind." Therefore, the Holy Spirit is the same as Jesus. The original Greek word for *comforter* means "one who is called to be alongside." Therefore, in being filled with God's Spirit, we have His sufficiency for every need we face.

God's Spirit, upon taking up residence in our lives, desires access into every area. It is in being alone that the Holy Spirit can fully impact us. This filling is not a passive act, but an active one. J. Oswald Sanders in his book *The Holy Spirit and His Gifts* has stated the concept well:

> The conception behind the command is not that of an empty vessel passively waiting for something to be poured into it, as water into an empty glass. A better illustration would be that of a house and its owner. The Holy Spirit is to occupy and control the life of the believer in whom he dwells and whom he fills just as the owner occupies and controls the house in which he lives.[2]

As we voluntarily surrender areas of our life to God, He fully takes control. When this occurs, it impacts and changes our attitudes, thoughts, words, and actions to be in conformity to the will of God as made known through His Word.

Does this mean that we will have more of the Holy Spirit than some others around us? No, Rene Pache poignantly sets forth the reality of what being filled with God's Spirit means. "From the start let us observe what has been frequently pointed out, that the fullness of the Spirit does not imply that *we* have more of the Spirit at our disposal but, to the contrary, that He possesses more of us and holds us entirely at His disposal."[3]

In case you are wondering how one can experience this filling of the Holy Spirit, let me share what I believe are the crucial elements of being filled with God's Spirit:

> <u>Desire the fullness of God in your life:</u> "Blessed are those who hunger and thirst for righteousness, for they will be filled" (Matthew 5:6).

> <u>Declare your need:</u> "Call to me and I will answer you and tell you great and unsearchable things you do not know" (Jeremiah 33:3).

> <u>Denounce sin in your life:</u> "If we confess our sins, he is faithful and just and will forgive us our sins and purify us from all unrighteousness" (1 John 1:9).

> <u>Determine to remain filled:</u> ". . . Be filled with the Spirit" (Ephesians 5:18).

Many Christians are living in self-imposed spiritual poverty. They find it easier to wait, plead, beg, and go through an extensive list of external conditions in an attempt to get God's Spirit. How ridiculous when all the time, it is as easy as a heart's desire and a simple prayer. Perhaps you may want to pray right now. Let me ask you to take a moment and bow your heart before the Father and submit a prayer something like this:

Heavenly Father, I love You. I admit that I have been controlling and directing my life. I have sinned against You and therefore know that I have grieved Your Holy Spirit. I claim forgiveness of that sin and ask for a fresh filling of Your

Spirit. I pray this in accordance to Your Word where You commanded me to be filled. Now I stake my faith on Your promise that You would do so if I ask in faith. I thank You for already filling my life and pray that You would make it everything for which You created it.

As you pray that prayer, be assured that God has heard it. Be assured also that He will answer it. The prayer that you've just prayed is directly in line with scriptural guidelines. As a result, God has promised, "This is the assurance we have in approaching God: that if we ask anything according to his will, he hears us. And if we know that he hears us—whatever we ask—we know that we have what we asked of him" (1 John 5:14, 15).

For Joseph, the Spirit of God was the indispensable ingredient that had taken him through the pits and then to the pinnacle. In the same way, God's Spirit is our indispensable ingredient. But remember, the key is not a question of how much of God's Spirit you have, but *how much of you God's Spirit has.*

POINTS TO PONDER

THE INDISPENSABLE INGREDIENT

1. What are some common misconceptions of the Holy Spirit?
2. What role did the Holy Spirit play in Joseph's life? How does it differ from the role He plays in our lives?
3. What does the Holy Spirit convict us of? How does He convict? Recall a specific example.
4. What fresh or "re-freshed" insights of the Holy Spirit did you gain in this story?
5. What steps can you take to allow the Holy Spirit to have a more dynamic role in your life?

9

The Marks of a True Leader

MAXIM:

A leader is not measured simply by who he leads, but by how he leads.

It's an amazing phenomenon. It is not characterized by uniformity. The views concerning it are not viewed with unanimity. It comes in all size packages—tall, short, fat, thin, charismatic, and quiet. Endless books have been written about it and videos produced depicting it. The phenomenon is leadership.

While flying back from a speaking engagement recently, I was reading *USA Today.* I came across two separate articles concerning two different men. Both are outstanding leaders in their own right, yet vastly different.

One had grown up in a middle-class background in Queens, New York. His mother was a schoolteacher and his father a lawyer. In college he majored in philosophy though his mother wanted him to be a doctor. Dropping out of medical school, he did a short hitch with the army and then chose a career on Wall Street.

He went to an uncle who loaned him $400,000 to buy a seat on the New York Stock Exchange. In doing so, he told his uncle that he planned to be one of the top businessmen in the country and asked the uncle if he wanted to join him. With a slight grin, the uncle passed on the "chance of a lifetime." Now the uncle could kick himself around the block.

Since 1978 Carl Icahn has collected close to $200 million in profits. He has become the chairman of Transworld Airlines and ACF Industries. Icahn is a perpetual-motion financial machine. At fifty he rarely takes a vacation and then only for a day or two at a time. Even on vacation, he is constantly on the phone dealing with business-related matters. He gave up golf because it took too much time away from work. In the heat of takeover battles, he may work straight through a day and into the next in his Manhattan office. His energy seems to be magically supplied from some unlimited power source.

The second man about whom I read has a different view, though just as successful. He is a forty-five-year-old business tycoon. He sleeps ten hours a night. When headaches come, he closes shop and goes home. After working on a large business deal, he may well take off for a week to go fishing. But in the process he has acquired controlling interest in twenty-one companies which employ 37,000 people with annual sales of nearly $2 billion. His name is Irwin Jacobs.

Unlike Icahn, Jacobs' work routine mirrors his flexibility. He doesn't run by a schedule. Often the calendar at his desk hasn't been turned for weeks. He has an easygoing manner which deceptively hides his whirlwind mind.

Regardless of personalities, industry would have to agree that both have been very successful. Yet both are so very different. And different leaders employ different methodologies. Perhaps you have found your own greatly differs from the majority of those around you or from Mr. Icahn and Mr. Jacobs.

However, while I am convinced that there is no one correct style of leadership, I am certain that there are key characteristics indispensable to strong leaders. The best leaders I know are the ones who know how to use different types and styles of leadership at different times in varying circumstances. But key characteristics that underlie leadership seem to be common to all outstanding leaders. These characteristics were mirrored in the life of Joseph.

Trustworthy. In a generation that has witnessed Watergate and the fiasco of Vietnam, trust seems to be a commodity which has been greatly devalued. Yet it is a quality essential for leadership.

In our day of constant change, people are looking for the anchor of reliability. Reliability is primarily based upon trust. We see this in the life of Joseph. Even though he was sold into slavery and served in Potiphar's household, Scripture relates that Potiphar made Joseph administrator of all he had. Scripture says, ". . . with Joseph in charge, he did not concern himself with anything except the food he ate" (Genesis 39:6). The same quality was again exhibited in Joseph while he was in prison when he was made responsible for all that was done there. "The warden paid no attention to anything under Joseph's care, because the Lord was with Joseph and gave him success in whatever he did" (39:23). Both men had great respect and trust for Joseph's leadership. The reason can be boiled down to the fact that they knew Joseph to be trustworthy. They could rely on his work and leadership. When he said something would be done, they knew to expect it. When he said he would take care of a problem, they knew it would be settled. Joseph's performance was consistent with both his word and his character.

Today there is a great need for the same quality. Trustworthiness is the bedrock on which leadership can be built. No one will look to a leader who cannot be depended upon. This means that truth must characterize everything a leader does.

Recently, I was visited by a friend. He is a business executive in sales and has been very successful. When speaking of one of the companies he represents, he was discussing its president. He commented that this gentlemen had one point of consistency, and that was his inconsistency. He went on to say that the difficulty expressed by many who worked for this gentleman was the fact that even his inconsistency was inconsistent. They could not rely on when he would change direction, switch to different products, change pricing structures, or completely alter strategies the company was taking. My friend shared that he grieved for the company because of the lack of trustworthiness in the leadership.

The Scripture says that God also desires ". . . truth in the inner parts . . ." (Psalms 51:6). But not only does God desire truth in our hearts, so do those for whom we work. Scripture says, "Kings take pleasure in honest lips; they value a man who speaks the truth" (Proverbs 16:13). This message is directed to everyone, for all of us answer to some authority. Without exception those to whom we are accountable look for honesty as a chief characteristic in us.

I recently heard of a business executive who brought in one of his employees to discuss a problem. The executive said, "I want an explanation and I want the truth." The employee responded, "Make up your mind. You can't have both." What a tragedy!

Several months ago I met Donald Seibert, former chairman of the board of the JCPenney Corporation. In our conversation I asked him what one quality he looked for more than any other when he employed people. Without hesitation, Don responded that he looked for integrity and trustworthiness. Perhaps that is why Oscar Wilde said, "If one tells the truth, one is sure sooner or later to be found out."

Perhaps you are thinking that this doesn't necessarily apply to you. Your job or responsibility may not be one of overwhelming importance involving millions of dollars or the administration of great estates. But Christ spoke directly to you and to me when He said, "Whoever can be trusted with very little can also be trusted with much, and whoever is dishonest with very little will also be dishonest with much" (Luke 16:10). How are you doing with that standard? How about the daily routine jobs that you do? Are you trustworthy and faithful in them? Are your reports done with excellence? Is your work at the office consistently reliable? Does your work at the plant reflect a deep commitment to Christ and truth in your inner being?

A true leader is trustworthy!

Visionary. "The world of a blind man is bounded by his touch; an ignorant man's world by the limits of his knowledge; a great man's world by the limits of his vision." Paul Harvey's words have made a lasting impression on me. In our day of rapidly increasing technology, a leader must have vision. In fact, Warren Bennis and Bert Nanus in their excellent book, *Leaders,* said, "Vision is the commodity of leaders."[1]

A true leader is not limited to the present in his vision. That is why Robert Kennedy caught our attention when he said, "Some men look at things as they are and ask, 'Why?' But I look at things as they could be and ask, 'Why not?' " For the leader the present is only a springboard to the future. But then perhaps that's why we don't have an overabundance of leaders. Too many become enslaved by the routine. The present becomes an incarceration of problems and circumstances rather than a passageway and preparation for opportunity.

Joseph was a man of vision. It began with the dreams of his

early childhood. Those God-given dreams created in him a sense of destiny. As I talk with young people today, too often it seems that a sense of destiny is missing from their lives. They are merely shuffling through routine. One of my dear friends, who is a leading spokesmen for youth ministry in the United States, says that the youth of the eighties may most correctly be characterized by one word—*apathy*. As one was overhead to say, "The chief problem with us as youth may be apathy—but who really cares?" One thing is for sure, no one who is apathetic can be a person of vision.

Joseph was anything but apathetic. Even in the midst of circumstances beyond his control, he continued to have a perspective characterized by vision. What do I mean by vision? I believe that vision is the ability to bring the internal perspective into the present condition. It is the ability to see and dream about what could be and not be shackled by what is. Through slavery, prison, disappointment, and failing friendship, Joseph retained his drive in a move toward God's calling upon his life.

Perhaps this is the very basis to which we need to return. God has a plan for each of us and for every organization. There is a dream which we are to fulfill. And it is only as we reach out with vision that the dream moves from being a possibility to a probability. That vision may be for your Sunday Bible Study class. It could be for a scout troop you lead. Perhaps it is for a church in which you serve or attend. Maybe it is for your job. Or perhaps for your home and family. Regardless of where it is, I pray that you have a vision.

The Bible says, "Where there is no vision, the people perish . . ." (Proverbs 29:18 KJV). The Hebrew word used for *perish* literally means to "become naked." A person without a vision and a dream is not in step with God and His design. That person is stripped of power for living. Though he or she may be involved in much religious activity, there are no lasting results. It becomes motion without meaning. And the person's defense against the spiritual Adversary is stripped away. Could that characterize you?

The New American Standard Bible translates the same verse as, "Where there is no vision, the people are unrestrained. . . ." This suggests the picture of unbridled horses that have never been tamed. When you lack vision, life becomes undisciplined, undirected, and ineffective. Could it be that those characteristics are ones with which you identify? There is no need to!

I believe that vision can be gained by anyone God desires to use in a leadership role. It is not some hidden mystery discernible to only a few. I believe the problem is that you and I go about gaining vision the wrong way. Too often we think it is some mystical dream which we have to conjure up. Biblically that is not how I see vision. I think too often we start at the wrong end. We begin with what we want to accomplish. A correct vision is based on the Person for whom we want to accomplish it.

In Scripture there are two great illustrations of proper vision. One is in Isaiah 6 and the other is about Peter as found in Luke 5. In both of these instances the men gained a vision that not only ignited their own lives but the lives of those around them. But look with me quickly at the steps that brought about that vision:

1. *They got a vision of God.* In each case they started with a fresh look at who God is. They saw anew His majesty and greatness and how much He loved them. They saw that in God there is absolutely no limit to His power and grace; and whatever they needed to live life successfully, they found in Him. God's Word indicates this when it says, "His divine power has given us everything we need for life and godliness . . ." (2 Peter 1:3). God, in His love for us, gives us everything we need for effective daily living as well as developing a godly character.

Isaiah saw God in the temple in quietness. Peter saw God afresh through Jesus, His Son, in a boat. These examples tell us that there is no special secret place where we must go to see God. Instead the key is to have the desire to see Him, blended with a pure, unselfish motive.

Blessed are those who hunger and thirst for righteousness, for they will be filled. . . . Blessed are the pure in heart, for they will see God.

Matthew 5:6, 8

Most often that fresh view of God and His sufficiency is best found in the quietness of our own private lives when it is just God and us. For some, however, it can come in a worship service or a Bible study. The location makes no difference. The desire on our part makes all the difference in the world. But what if God seems remote or far from you in recent days? Just remember that it is not God who has moved. He is in the same place He's always been. He is near and waiting for you to come back and spend time with Him—to see Him as He really is. That requires that we seek Him. David gave this advice to his son, Solomon.

And you, my son Solomon, acknowledge the God of your father, and serve him with wholehearted devotion and with a willing mind, for the Lord searches every heart and understands every motive behind the thoughts. If you seek him, he will be found by you. . . .

1 Chronicles 28:9

Isaiah speaks more directly to you and me when he says:

Seek the Lord while he may be found;
    call on him while he is near.
Let the wicked forsake his way
    and the evil man his thoughts.
Let him turn to the Lord, and he will
    have mercy on him.
and to our God, for he will freely pardon.

Isaiah 55:6, 7

Perhaps you are having difficulty at this particular time, even desiring to have a fresh vision of God. All of us go through those times. If that is the case in your life, let me encourage you to be honest with God. He knows your heart anyway. Admit to Him that you are having difficulty. Honestly proclaim that at this particular time you don't have a desire for a vision and are not sure you are going to want one in the near future. At the same time, willingly admit that you know the attitude is not right. Therefore, ask God to change your attitude. You will be amazed at what God will begin to do if you are willing to allow Him to mold your will in accordance with His desire. Perhaps right now your best prayer would be . . .

Lord, make me willing to be willing.

2. *They had a vision of themselves.* Isaiah quickly saw his sinfulness when He saw God's holiness. Peter, likewise, immediately told Christ to leave him because he was not worthy of being in the Lord's presence. That is a common reaction when we see God in a new light. We realize that on our own merit, we have absolutely no worth or merit with which to earn a right standing with God or His favor.

The outstanding Christian leader D. L. Moody was once asked who gave him the greatest difficulty in carrying out his ministry. Without hesitation, Mr. Moody responded, "That's easy. There is only one person who gives me more frustration and difficulty than anyone else—D. L. Moody." Though we esteem a man like Moody as a Christian leader and tend to place him on a pedestal, he exhibited rare insight. Moody understood that we are our own worst enemy. Understanding that fact can help us be much more effective in coping with daily living. We immediately see that our difficulties and problems aren't normally caused by other people, circumstances, or the wrong breaks.

When we experience a fresh touch of God in our lives, we

inevitably have an immediate recognition of our sinfulness in His presence. The closer we come to His light, the darker our own sin looks. You will know you've received such a look at God when you respond to yourself as Peter and Isaiah did.

3. *They had a vision of their call.* We want to start with a vision of what special thing God has for us to do. Unfortunately, our priorities are out of order when we do that. Our lives must be recorded and brought into right relationship with God before we can be usable in His hand. Once we have gained that renewed sense of His presence and sovereignty in our lives and have willingly submitted to His leadership, He shows us the things He wants us to do. We would do well to remember that being always comes before doing. Thomas Edison said, "There is much more opportunity than there are people to see it." Those of us who see opportunity are those who have vision. And for a Christian to have vision, he must see God, himself, and his life's goal in proper order. So remember,

A task without a vision is drudgery
A vision without a task is a dream
A vision wedded with a task is destiny.

A sensitivity for people. Of all the skills most important to a leader, there is none that exceeds relating well with people. John D. Rockefeller said that he would pay more for that ability than any other quality in an executive. Rockefeller understood that the greatest asset of any organization is its people. Therefore, it is critical that leaders be able to deal with the chief asset of an organization.

It seems unfortunate to me that in all the emphasis on management today, the management of people is not always at the forefront. Often the technical aspects of managment are espoused to the neglect of people management. One may be able to balance the company books while demoralizing the people.

Joseph constantly showed a sensitivity for those around him. He was always looking for ways to help and to serve others.

As a young man of seventeen, he helped in the family business.

As Potiphar's administrator, he effectively managed his entire estate.

When he could have turned the tables on Potiphar's wife with accusation, he kept quiet.

In prison he proved himself trustworthy.

While serving his term, he went out of his way to help the cupbearer and the baker by interpreting their dreams.

Not knowing what the reaction would be, he boldly interpreted Pharaoh's dream.

Having been rewarded by Pharaoh and made prime minister, he found great favor with the people of Egypt.

Rather than seek retribution, he helped his brothers and their families survive the famine.

His orientation was to give his best to people and bring out the best in others.

I am reminded of Douglas MacArthur. MacArthur was renowned for giving his best to his men. In return they gave their best to MacArthur. The loyalty they exhibited toward the man was fierce. They not only lived for him, they died for him. William Manchester, in his book *American Caesar*, says it was because the men knew MacArthur adored them. His love was evident and his concern for people obvious. That will always elicit loyalty.

When I left seminary, I had the opportunity to go on staff at a very large church in Texas. The pastor was fairly new himself and had been one of my seminary professors. His name was Dr. Bill Pinson.

I'll never forget being interviewed for the job. We went through a great number of meetings. At the end of a long weekend, we were sitting in the banquet room of a local restaurant. My wife and I were seated with the church's personnel committee, Dr. and Mrs. Pinson, and their family. As we ate, we discussed many details, covering as much ground as possible in a short time. Right in the middle of our lunch and conversation, Bill's eight-year-old daughter interrupted by saying, "Daddy, I had the greatest dream last night!"

Expecting Bill to tell her to be quiet and to please remain seated for a little while, I was stunned with his response. He turned to Allison and looking fully into her eyes said, "Honey, tell me about your dream." For those few moments, the world of interviews, church life, and future decisions stood still. No one was more important to Bill at that time than his little girl. I sat amazed at the lesson I was being taught by this man: There is nothing more important than people. Regardless of how small, every person is of the utmost importance and deserves love and attention.

The two years that I spent working under the leadership of Dr. Pinson were two of the finest in my career. I was to find that he did not react that way merely to his young daughter. After having been on staff at the church for only six months, I received a letter at home. It had been written from a hotel out of state. It was a note from Bill. In it he said that as he reviewed the exciting things that had happened in his life in the last year, he counted the opportunity for us to work together among the top events. This was a man who was being invited to speak all over the world and yet he had taken time to write a personal note to me affirming me and encouraging me for the future.

The first time I preached for him when he was out of town, I remember sitting in the study at church in final preparation. The phone rang. As I picked it up, a familiar voice said, "How are you doing? I just wanted you to know that I'm praying for you." It was Bill again. He was calling from the Midwest just to let me know he was with me in spirit.

I've seen the man go on later to serve as the president of Golden Gate Baptist Theological Seminary in San Francisco. I've heard a large number of compliments to the outstanding job he did while serving there. He is now the executive director of the Texas Baptist Convention. It is the largest Southern Baptist state convention in our country. Again, he is leading and setting a pace to which the other states look for guidance and example. Today within my heart and mind still reside the lessons Bill Pinson taught me. A team works best when they know they are loved and appreciated. You can demand an immense amount of work from people who know that they are affirmed and are important. When they know they are a critical part of the team and are appreciated and loved by the leader, they will charge hell with a water pistol.

That was the kind of man Joseph was. He was always putting others before himself. Perhaps Paul sets forth that type of leadership best when he tells the Church in Thessalonica, ". . . we were gentle among you, like a mother caring for her little children. We loved you so much that we were delighted to share with you not only the gospel of God but our lives as well, because you had become so dear to us" (1 Thessalonians 2:7, 8). How does a mother love her children? She loves them sacrificially—not just when it's convenient. How many times does a mother get up in the middle of the night to hold a sick child in her arms? Or get a glass of water for one who is thirsty? Or pull into her lap a child who is filthy from play but who has skinned his knee, in order to comfort him? Yes, a mother loves regardless of the inconvenience. The child is most important, for it is the wise mother who knows that affirmation and love build the self-esteem and confidence so necessary in the heart of the youngster. So it is with a leader. The leader loves regardless of circumstances. He is always looking at what can be done to help the other person. He is giving his life away. That's what Paul meant when he said, "We were delighted to share with you not only the gospel of God *but our lives as well.* . . ."

But Paul didn't stop there. He went on to say, "You know that we dealt with each of you as a father deals with his own children, encouraging, comforting and urging you to live lives worthy of God, who calls you into his kingdom and glory" (vv. 11, 12). The wise leader also loves like a father. For concern is not enough. There must also be encouraging and motivating. The leader challenges others to rise to their highest potential. And you don't have to be a corporate executive to do that in the life of another.

I remember the book by Christine Sparks entitled *The Elephant Man.* It highlights the importance of believing in and motivating other people. You remember that the chief character was the hideously deformed victim of neurofibromatosis. John Merrick was so grotesque that he qualified for a second-rate circus. Becoming ill, he was rescued by a physician and placed in a London hospital. His story ran in the London *Times.* It caught public attention. Madge Kendall, the leading actress of the day and incomparably beautiful, learned of the Elephant Man through the media. For some strange reason she was compelled to visit him. Taking a gift, the complete works of William Shakespeare, she entered his room. Merrick opened the heavy volume to *Romeo and Juliet.*

Quietly he began to read aloud. As if on cue, Madge Kendall responded, reading Juliet's lines. Moved with encouragement and compassion, she gently kissed the corner of his mouth.

"Why, Mr. Merrick, you're not the Elephant Man at all."

"Oh . . . no?"

"Oh, no, no, no . . . you're Romeo."

With that the Elephant Man's conversion began, from an "it" to a person.

The true leader helps others rise to meet their potential.

Disciplined. A true leader doesn't give up. So it was with Joseph. Often it would have been so easy to throw in the towel. At every turn he seemed to have run into a brick wall. It seemed his life went uphill with the brakes on. And just about the time he thought the wind had shifted to his back, a hurricane would catch him from the blind side. But did he give up? Not on your life.

The characteristic of discipline begins with the conquering of one's self. That is what Paul meant hundreds of years later when he wrote, "The fruit of the Spirit is love, joy, peace, patience, kindness, goodness, faithfulness, gentleness and *self-control*" (Galatians 5:22, 23, *italics mine*). We could buy the entire list if he could have just left off "self-control." Why did he have to add that? It definitely doesn't make your day, does it?

I've found that to have self-control is not as easy as making a decision. In fact, I've found a big difference between making a decision and a commitment. Decisions are something that we can make based on facts at hand. The problem is that they can change tomorrow. A commitment, on the other hand, requires follow-through. It is the long-term side of decision. And self-control takes commitment.

Let me share with you what I mean. Have you ever decided to go on a diet? In your mind you are convinced that you could do it. You picture the slim, trim figure you would be in a matter of weeks. Look out world! And then you happen to be with someone who orders a hot fudge sundae. That is the test. Is it simply a decision or is it a commitment? If you follow through, you have commitment. Self-control. But if you give in, then all you have is a decision.

"Therefore, my dear brothers, stand firm. Let nothing move you. Always give yourselves fully to the work of the Lord, because you know that your labor in the Lord is not in vain" (1 Corinthians 15:58). A leader stands firm. He doesn't look for the easy way out. He doesn't let momentary desires or whims move him. He hangs tough. Anybody can quit. It takes a leader "to take a lickin' and keep on tickin'."

There is a humorous illustration that comes out of John F. Kennedy's presidential campaign of 1960. After a moving and dynamic speech in San Antonio, Texas, to a large, enthusiastic crowd at the Alamo, Kennedy wanted to make a quick exit. He realized that this was the memorial ground for a handful of courageous Texans who had held off a large Mexican army. Turning to Maury Maverick, a local politician, he said, "Maury, let's get out of here. This is getting to me. Where's the back door?" With a rapier wit, Maury replied, "Senator, if there had been a back door in the Alamo, there wouldn't have been any heroes." Leaders don't look for the back doors. How about you?

Decisiveness. One of the greatest difficulties in life can be making decisions—especially the major ones.

Deciding to leave the noise, traffic, and hustle of the city behind, a family headed for the wide open spaces. Their goal was to start a cattle ranch. Having purchased a large amount of acreage, this family soon settled down to their task.

Some friends came to visit and were fascinated with the operation. Walking across one of the pastures, a friend asked the name of the place. The head of the house responded, "Well, I wanted to call it the Flying-W but my wife wanted to name it the Suzie-Q. Then one of our sons said that he liked the Bar-J. But the other son preferred the Lazy-Y. So we compromised and we call it the Flying-W/Suzie-Q/Bar-J/Lazy-Y."

The visitor nodded his head. "But where are all the cattle?"

"None of them survived the branding!" replied the rancher.

Though decisions are not always easy, they are a must for the leader. And in making them, not everybody will be happy.

Joseph was decisive. When faced with the prospect of future famine, Joseph challenged the Pharaoh:

Now let the Pharaoh look for a discerning and wise man and put him in charge of the land of Egypt. Let Pharaoh appoint commissioners over the land to take a fifth of the harvest of Egypt during the seven years of abundance. They should collect all the food of these good years that are coming and store up the grain under the authority of Pharaoh, to be kept in the cities for food. This food should be held in reserve for the country, to be used during the seven years of famine that will come upon Egypt, so that the country may not be ruined by the famine.

Genesis 41:33–36

Joseph had taken the bull by the horns. He saw the upcoming problem and set forth a proposal to cope with it. He was not an airhead with both feet firmly planted five feet off the ground. Instead he was willing to put himself on the line and make a recommendation. He had no guarantee that it was the perfect decision and that everything would go well, but he knew something had to be done.

One of the greatest cop-outs I hear in the ranks of leadership is, "I don't have a plan. I know God's in control. " The fact that God is in control is a given. Yet throughout history, God has used men and women to chart the course and to set forth the plan. Granted. God directs men in choosing the right decision, but He puts the decision in *their hands.*

God's Word tells us, "Where is the man who fears the Lord? God will teach him how to choose the best" (Psalms 25:12 TLB). Notice it says that God shows "him" how to choose. Proverbs 24:4 reiterates this fact when it says, "Any enterprise is built by wise planning, becomes strong through common sense, and profits wonderfully by keeping abreast of the facts" (TLB). Decisions are not a luxury, they are a necessity. You will find that an ounce of forethought is worth more than a ton of afterthought.

Joseph followed well the task of a leader. Many organizations I know use a simple acrostic to describe their decision process.

Plan
Organize
Lead
Evaluate

Joseph saw the problem and immediately devised a plan to tackle it. He then followed through by organizing to carry out the plan. Resources had to be marshaled. Responsibilities delegated. People enlisted.

Then he led. "During the seven years of abundance the land produced plentifully. Joseph collected all the food produced in those seven years of abundance in Egypt and stored it in the cities. In each city he put the food grown in the fields surrounding it. Joseph stored up huge quantities of grain, like the sand of the sea; it was so much that he stopped keeping records because it was beyond measure" (Genesis 41:47–49). For seven years the plan was put into action. The leader followed through to translate from paper and pencil into reality.

Without doubt, evaluation was done along the way. In fact, the Scripture indicates that records were well kept, and those records reflected so much grain in storage that they were able to stop the program.

By the way, if you think it was easy making a decision, remember when the decision was made. Joseph had proposed a storage and rationing time seven years prior to the famine. Do you think that was met with wild enthusiasm by the people? How do you think it would be met in our day? Joseph realized that sometimes the shoes of leadership are the shoes of loneliness. There is no guarantee that once a decision is made, it will be heartily endorsed by everyone concerned. But a key distinction of a leader is that he does not only look for what is easy and pragmatic, he looks primarily for what is right. And when it's right, he acts.

One last word of caution. Decisiveness does not guarantee a lack of mistakes. In our day we seem to have the false notion that we can gain some magical ability to be decisive and successful and therefore not make mistakes in the process. When a major league batter hits in excess of .300, he has had an outstanding year. If an NFL quarterback has a 60 percent completion record, he's had a great year. Why is it that we think that we should be throwing touchdown passes 100 percent of the time? We must remember that sometimes a noble failure serves in just as great a way as a distinguished success.

One of the most insightful stories that always brings a smile to my face is of the young vice-president who had just been chosen as the president-elect of a major financial institution. Never in the history of the bank had such a young man been chosen to steer its future. Overwhelmed, and yet desiring to be the best he could be, he made an appointment with the retiring president.

Within the scope of their meeting, the young executive queried the experienced leader with, "Sir, I have admired your leadership of our institution for a number of years. It has been one of tremendous success. One of the key questions I'd like to ask, for my own growth and knowledge, is how have you done it?"

With a sparkle in his eye the senior executive replied, "It's really quite simple. I can sum up the answer in two words—*good decisions*."

A bit unsettled, the newly elected president, seeking clarification, asked, "But how did you learn to make good decisions?"

With a smile the elder statesman replied, "I can rap that up in one word—*experience*."

Still seeking for a handle onto which he could grasp, the young man asked a final question. "But how did you gain the experience?"

"Easy," replied the retiring president. "By making bad decisions."

Without exception, you will have your share of bad decisions. But you will make the choice as to what happens. You will either learn from them and gain your own experience upon which you will base future good decisions, or you will retreat from decision making and therefore become ineffective. You will make the choice.

May God raise up leaders like Joseph in our day. Who knows, perhaps there is a key area where He needs you to lead. At work. At home. Perhaps a Bible study class. Whatever it may be, I challenge you to rise to be a leader. Do it in your own style and with your own personality, but be sure these characteristics are incorporated in your life.

POINTS TO PONDER

THE MARKS OF A TRUE LEADER

1. Of the different qualities of leadership discussed in this chapter, which did you find most helpful to you? Why?
2. In the illustrations of Isaiah and Joseph, what did you discover that can be helpful in your life? How can you best implement these principles in daily living?
3. Think back and remember a leader, boss, coach, parent who has encouraged you to rise to your best. What did it mean in your life? Determine someone for whom you could do the same and commit to begin this week by encouraging them to be all that they have the ability to be.
4. What area of life do you have the greatest difficulty bringing under discipline? Why? What can be done to bring it under control?
5. Analyze why it is so difficult for many to be decisive. What do you see to be the major roadblocks? Determine what you feel are some helpful guidelines to effective decision making.

10
Moving in the Flow of God's Will

It happened early one cold December morning in 1944. Parachutes billowed in the sky over Europe. Quietly men descended to the ground suspended like puppets on strings. But puppets they were not.

The Allied offensive, which was six months old, had moved with precision across Europe. It would soon come to a halt, however. These soldiers from the sky were German soldiers. They carried no weapons. Their uniforms were American. Along with them, suspended under numerous parachutes, came American Jeeps. They were descending behind Allied lines. A defensive move that was brilliant in its origin was being implemented by the leaders of the Third Reich. The mission of these soldiers was to travel the roads of the advancing Allied armies and change all signs. If the signposts were turned to give wrong directions, the Allied forces would be not only confused but oftentimes lost in the surrounding countryside. Needed reinforcements would be unduly delayed. Allied troops caught in heated battle would wonder what was keeping the reinforcements.

The shattering reality is that the strategy almost succeeded. Had it not been discovered, the war may have been delayed indefinitely. Who knows, perhaps the whole outcome would have been different.

Today the signposts of our society are being changed in similar fashion. Others have simply been torn down—moral signposts, theological signposts, and ethical signposts. What used to be black-and-white issues are now called gray. As a result, many people are searching for an anchoring point to grant stability in their daily living. Many are searching for reality behind the facade of beauty, brains, and bucks. Questions abound and answers seem few.

All of us want to know our purpose in life. For those of us who call ourselves Christians, the question goes further. We want to know, "How do I determine God's will for my life?" Even if we believe that we understand some of the principles of knowing God's will, there tends to be a perennial questioning of how to stay in the center of it. Evidently Joseph had found the secret.

Joseph now was in his early thirties. Though a relatively young man, it seemed as though he had lived multiple lifetimes in the previous years. Those years had seen the pinnacles of accomplishment, only to be followed by the depths of disaster. Through his myriad experiences, however, Joseph had found the flow of God's will. As he reflected upon his life, he could see God's hand at every juncture.

Perhaps Joseph perceived things a bit more clearly than we do. So many of us see but few really understand the true challenge of our lives. We also tend to get the cart before the horse. Our main concern centers on what God wants us to *do* with our lives. Joseph understood that our first concern should be what God wants us to *be!* It is only at the point of being what God wants us to be that He reveals what He wants us to do. *Being* precedes *doing.* Joseph had spent his life cultivating a godly character in order that he might find his preordained place of service.

One of the key principles of life is that in order to know what God desires to do *with* your life requires a commitment to God *of* your life. That is easy to say. But what type of commitment leads us to be what God wants us to be in order that we might accomplish what He wants us to do? We are in a much better position than Joseph to answer that question. God clearly displays how we can know His will in His Word. Let's jump ahead to the completion of the Old Testament—the New Testament—and see what God has to say to us concerning finding the flow of His will. It is there that we will find how the Josephs of today can be assured of God's total control of their lives.

No place is the understanding of God's will better depicted than in Romans 12:1, 2. There the Apostle Paul who, like Joseph, had sought godly character, says,

> Therefore, I urge you, brothers, in view of God's mercy, to offer your bodies as living sacrifices, holy and pleasing to God—which is your spiritual worship. Do not conform any longer to the pattern of this world, but be transformed by the renewing of your mind. Then you will be able to test and approve what God's will is—his good, pleasing and perfect will.

The Basis of Commitment

Paul has just finished the first eleven chapters of the magnificent Book of Romans. He has discussed what God has accomplished for the believer. Now he shifts gears from principle to practice.

You and I are called to a commitment to both know God and live according to His will. Paul, realizing the importance of this complete commitment, challenges us by saying, "I urge you, brothers" to make such a decision. The picture he paints in these words in the original language is that of a brother putting his arm around another to both comfort and plead. As one friend to another, he is entreating us to seriously consider following through with the challenge he is setting forth.

If we are to make such a total surrender, Paul is aware that we must have a viable basis for doing so. That basis is what God has already done for us. Paul has established that in the first eleven chapters.

Paul began by painting the tragic portrait of man separated from God. This was man's own doing. God, from the beginning, gave man every evidence of the existence of a divine Creator and His love for man. "For since the creation of the world God's invisible qualities—his eternal power and divine nature—have been clearly seen, being understood from what has been made, so that men are without excuse" (Romans 1:20).

Man is constantly making excuses. You have probably heard that an excuse is merely the skin of a reason stuffed with a lie. It has been happening ever since Adam said, "The woman you put here with me—she gave me some fruit from the tree, and I ate it" (Genesis 3:12). And so it goes. Today we still make excuses. We look for someone or something to blame. All along the problem is really deep within us.

Despite God's revelation of Himself through creation, man ". . . neither glorified him as God nor gave thanks to him, but their thinking became futile and their foolish hearts were darkened" (Romans 1:21). They began to serve the creature more than the Creator.

As though God's natural revelation was not enough, He also revealed Himself through men's consciences. Paul indicated that "... the requirements of the law are written on their hearts, their consciences also bearing witness, and their thoughts now accusing, now even defending them" (Romans 2:15). God placed as the inner guardian of men His guidelines of right and wrong.

Finally God revealed Himself thoroughly in His Son, Jesus Christ. "But now a righteousness from God, apart from law, has been made known, to which the Law and the Prophets testify. This righteousness from God comes through faith in Jesus Christ to all who believe ..." (Romans 3:21, 22). It was through Christ that God entered into the world, searching for man. Whereas all other religions find man seeking God, Christianity finds God reaching out to man.

Regardless of these efforts made by the Father, man continued to go his own way. The Bible refers to this mind-set as sin. It is basically a rebellion against God's will and direction for life and determination to do our own thing.

Scripture helps us to see that sin is not limited to the "biggies"—adultery, stealing, murder. Rather it is revealed in the everyday attitudes and actions of life:

Sin is anything we do that doesn't please God (1 John 3:4)
Sin is anything we think that doesn't please God (Proverbs 14:10; Matthew 15:16–20)
Sin is anything we say that doesn't please God (Matthew 12:36, 37)
Sin is anything we know that we should do but refuse to do (James 4:17)

In reading these have you noticed that what we often refer to as faults or personality deficiencies, God calls sin?

With this definition of sin, all of us would have to admit that we are sinners. The Bible couldn't agree more when it says, "All have sinned and fall short of the glory of God" (Romans 3:23). We all stand guilty due to the fact that God is not like a schoolteacher— He does not grade on a curve. If it were possible to earn our way to God, we could earn it only in one way and that would be perfection. You and I would have to live without breaking one scriptural guideline for living. Obedience would have to mark our every action, thought, and word. God says, "Whoever keeps the whole law and yet stumbles at just one point is guilty of breaking all of it" (James 2:10).

Stop and think a moment. Life is not much different. You don't have to rob a bank or commit murder to break the laws of our land. We are guilty of breaking the law even when we exceed the speed limit. Perhaps in our minds it is a difference in degree, but the law has still been broken. In the same way, since it is impossible for us to keep every one of God's commandments, we stand guilty!

But God has provided a solution. Paul went on to say that "the wages of sin is death [eternal separation from God], but the gift of God is eternal life in Christ Jesus our Lord" (Romans 6:23). That means it is nothing we can earn or deserve but instead must be accepted as a gift.

God's love and the gift of eternal life are freely available. When a person receives eternal life by receiving Christ as Savior, he becomes justified through faith. The word *justified* indicates both being made just as if we'd never sinned as well as having a brand-new character of life infused in us (Romans 5:1-11). As a result of that change, we become victors in life. Paul tells us that nothing that occurs can ever separate us again from the love of God made known through Christ (Romans 8:37-39).

So Paul has painted the incredible picture of what God has done on our behalf. After one has sacrificed so much and given so freely, why would anyone not wish to respond with appreciation and trust? Thus, Paul has established the basis of commitment. He has shown us that God has made the ultimate sacrifice for each one of us. Now He expects in return that we would openly commit our lives to His leadership in order that we might find His divine will. Have you made this initial commitment in your own life? Have you realized the great gift God has given you? By simple faith, have you asked Christ into your heart as Savior? Just think how fortunate you are. Joseph never had this complete truth!

If you have not had the joy or taken the opportunity to make this commitment in your life, why not do it now? It can be done with a single prayer. God is more concerned with your heart and your attitude than He is with your words. If you would like a suggestion on how to make this commitment, you might wish to pray the following prayer:

Heavenly Father, thank You for offering the gift of eternal life. Thank You for sending Your Son, Jesus, to die on the cross for my sins. I know I am a sinner and cannot save myself. I open the door of my life to receive Christ as my Savior and Lord. I put my complete trust in Him alone for eternal life. Please take control of my life and my future. Make me the person You created me to become.

If this expresses the desire of your heart, God has promised He will take up residence there. He will also never vacate the premises. He is there to stay.

This commitment doesn't depend merely on how you feel. Feelings are a false barometer for spiritual life. Instead, the assurance of eternal life is based on the fact of God's Word. He has written concerning His Word, "I write these things to you who believe in the name of the Son of God so that you may *know* that you have eternal life" (1 John 5:13, *italics mine*).

If you have prayed a prayer like the one given above, you must claim your faith on the fact of God's Word rather than on your feelings. Having made that commitment, the Bible says that you have eternal life. It doesn't say you "may have" but that you "have" (a present reality).

The Character of Commitment

Paul moves on, having laid the foundation of God's call upon our lives, to describe the kind of commitment we are asked to make. Paul challenges us to ". . . offer your bodies as living sacrifices, holy and pleasing to God—which is your spiritual worship" (Romans 12:1). The word used for *offer* is one that indicates a once-and-for-all commitment. We are to decide once and for all to yield, surrender, and place our lives at the disposal of Another. The character of that commitment is twofold: voluntary and complete.

First of all, Paul tells us that we are to offer our own bodies. Notice it is not something someone else can decide for us. Simply being raised in a home which participated in church activity does not indicate that you have made a Christian commitment such as Paul describes. Sitting under a gifted Bible teacher does not guarantee that the Bible has become a reality in your life in the area of surrender. No one else can do it for you—not your spouse, your parents, your friends, or your children. It is a personal decision and commitment that you must make for yourself.

Paul emphasizes the personal nature of the commitment in Romans 10:9, 10 when he says, "If *you* confess with *your* mouth, 'Jesus is Lord,' and believe in *your* heart that God raised him from the dead, *you* will be saved. For it is with *your* heart that *you* believe and are justified, and it is with *your* mouth that *you* confess and are saved" (*italics mine*). Notice how many times the words *you* and *your* are used. Paul was driving home the fact that you and I determine what is done with our own lives.

Second, Paul goes on to indicate that the commitment to God's will must be complete. He challenges us: "Offer your bodies as living sacrifices, holy and pleasing to God. . . ." When Paul speaks of our bodies, does he refer simply to our physical corporeal nature? Hardly. He was using the term to represent everything we are—our thoughts, intents, goals, and dreams, as well as our physical bodies.

When Paul referred to offering ourselves as a living sacrifice, many scholars feel he probably had in mind the burnt offering of the Old Testament. This was one of the most valuable of religious sacrifices for God's people. There were two classes of offering, those for reconciliation due to sin and those for consecration or commitment. The burnt offering was an offering of the latter type. It indicated a total commitment. This offering could be given by any Jew and signified his total abandonment to the will of God for his life.

Leviticus gives us some helpful insight into the burnt offering. It was first of all a *sweet savour offering*. This type of offering was made on the brazen altar in the court of the Tabernacle. Second, for this type of offering the sin of the offerer was not the emphasis, but rather his commitment and acceptance as a worshiper. The sweet savour signfied giving an offering to God that was so pleasing to Him that it would be satisfactorily acceptable. It fulfilled the loving and holy requirement for a fully committed life.

Third, when the burnt offering was given, it was of particular importance in that it was a life being offered on the altar. God had always claimed the life of His creation as His rightful possession. The life of the animal offered in the burnt offering, therefore, was symbolic of what is rightfully owed to God. It is indeed our highest form of worship.

Fourth, the offering was to be wholly burned upon the altar. The meat and peace offerings, on the other hand, were only partly burned with fire. Even sin offerings which were wholly burned were not burned on the altar. The burnt offering alone represented the duty of man entirely surrendering his all to his Creator.

From the burnt offering "the head" represented one's thoughts; "the legs" were symbolic of his spiritual walk; "the entrails" pictured one's feelings, emotions, and affections. It was a beautiful picture of God's wanting to be Lord of all or not at all. God did not ask for a partial commitment.

In our home I have always had a place to study and research. It often resembles the aftermath of a hurricane or nuclear war. Books are strewn throughout the room, papers are piled high, and project folders are scattered everywhere.

When someone knocks at the door or rings the doorbell, there is a typical pattern that occurs. I hear my wife, Cheryl, make a beeline for my study. There is the creaking of the door closing and finally the thump of its being secured. Then she quickly straightens herself up, walks to the door, and graciously opens it. The last thing she wants anyone to see is my study lest its totally unkempt nature reflect upon the rest of the house. It is the one area that I do not allow her access to for cleaning and straightening.

So it is with many of our lives. We can look "together" and confident on the outside while there is an area internally that has not been turned over to the Lordship of Christ. For some of us it is career and dreams. For others it can be a person or a possession. Whatever it may be that we are holding back, it hinders our commitment from being complete. God demands that our lives be surrendered to His control.

In allowing God complete access to our lives, we also make it possible for our "living sacrifice" to be "holy and pleasing to God." Our lives will be distinguished as being set apart for God's use. The principles by which we are striving to live will be those such as the ones found in the Sermon on the Mount (Matthew, chaps. 5–7). There will be realization that attitudes can be just as devastating as actions.

Paul tells us that in making such a commitment that is both voluntary and complete, we offer the highest form of worship. True spiritual worship is the offering of everyday life to God. Nothing is seen as too menial or insignificant to be a worship offering to Him. This new perspective allows us to see the world as God's temple and every act as an opportunity for service. Perhaps Ruth Graham captured the essence of this truth when she placed over the sink in her kitchen a sign which reads, SERVICE RENDERED HERE THREE TIMES DAILY. Mrs. Graham realizes that true commitment is not done most often in some spectacular moment but rather in the ordinary, everyday actions of life.

Barclay summarizes Paul's challenge: "Take your body; take all the tasks that you do everyday; take the ordinary work of the shop, the factory, the shipyard, the mine; and offer all that as an act of worship to God."[1] He goes on to say, "Real worship is the offering of everyday life to God."[2]

The Interpreter's Bible adds:

The new life is the life which has been sacrificed—offered to God. We cease to live to or for ourselves; we are under obligation to serve God in all we are and do. The truest sacrifice therefore is to live according to God's will. It might seem—when seen from one point of view—that the new life is lived under vigorous constraint; but Paul is never weary of repeating that the truest freedom is found only in the most unquestioning service of God. We may be under obligation, but this is the secret of Liberty.[3]

Dr. Robert Boyd Munger beautifully illustrated both characteristics of commitment in his famous sermon "My Heart Is Christ's Home." In it he equated his life to a house. Having invited Christ into his life, a household management inventory began. Thought life and intellect were seen as the library. The dining room depicted his appetites and desires in life. Friendships, activities, and amusements—the social side of life—were represented as the rumpus room, a room too often void of Christ's influence. Christ con-

185

tinued the inventory with the workroom. What lasting work was being produced for the Kingdom in this vital area of life?

Pointedly Munger revealed the areas of his life (house) that were being held back from Christ's management. Great vulnerability was shown as he identified with most of us. Finally he ended with a conversation between himself and Christ. That conversation summarized the character of commitment:

> A thought came to me. "Lord, is there any chance that you would take over the management of the whole house and operate it for me? . . . Would you take the responsibility to keep my life what it ought to be?"
>
> His face lighted up as he replied, "Certainly, that is what I want to do . . . but I am just a guest. I have no authority to proceed, since the property is not mine."[4]

The choice is ours. Are we willing to surrender all areas of life to His Lordship? The business? Family relationships? Social life? Appetites and desires? Will we grant Him the authority to proceed?

Have you voluntarily committed your life to God's control? Have you given Him every area of it? Are there areas which you are holding back? If so, you can never really truly know His will for your life's service if you are not following through with His will for your character.

Demand of Commitment

Not wanting to set forth an oversimplified call to commitment, Paul does not hedge on the demands made on one's life. As there was a twofold character of commitment, so there is a twofold demand of commitment. There is both a negative side and a positive side. Paul sets forth the negative aspect first when he says, "Do not conform any longer to the pattern of this world . . ." (Romans 12:2).

Perhaps J. B. Phillips best captured it when he translated this to read, "Don't let the world around you squeeze you into its own mould." We are told to steer clear of the world's superficial value system which places a premium on nonbiblical character qualities. The world emphasizes sensuality, off-grade humor, power, status, and wealth.

If we do not take great care, we may find ourselves in a similar position. Perhaps most dangerous, we can find ourselves moving schizophrenically between a Christian character and a character no different from the world around us. We adapt to the environment in which we find ourselves and then act accordingly. Rather than being a thermostat in setting the environment around us, we become more like a thermometer and simply react to circumstances and people.

When I was in second grade, a fad swept our school. Chameleon lizards were in vogue. You could take two dollars to the pet store and purchase your very own chameleon. Upon arriving home you would get a twelve-inch piece of yarn from your mother and tie one end around a safety pin. The other end would be tied very carefully around the neck of the chameleon—if it was not done carefully, you would be out another two dollars. We would then take our pets pinned to our blouses and shirts everywhere we went. Experience brought creativity. We began planning our wardrobes. When I wore a green shirt, I would coordinate with those around me to wear different shades of green or brown. When the teacher failed to hold our interest (which was most of the time), we would begin to change chameleons. We would watch the amazing transformation of their skin color from greens to browns and from browns to greens, depending upon the color of clothing we were wearing.

Then the shirt industry did the most unkind thing to the chameleon kingdom. It popularized madras plaids! Have you ever seen a chameleon try to match a plaid?

Unfortunately if we are not careful, we can become too much

like the chameleon. Paul tells us to avoid that at all costs. Pressures to conform come from every quarter. One can be forced to conform in several ways. Paul Tillich warned:

We may be conformists not only if we agree but also if we disagree, and we may be non-conformist, not only if we disagree but also if we agree. These are warning words against those of us who believe that their revolutionary impetus liberates them from the danger of conformism. But it does not.[5]

In the same manner one can become conformed to a church, a policy, a stance, or any other element in life. Perhaps the most dangerous conformation is to our own views. We may become so ingrained in our prejudices, attitudes, and behaviors that we are unwilling to bend. Opposing views are ignored. Paul warns, "Steer clear! Beware."

On the other hand, there is a positive demand of commitment. Commitment of our lives to God demands change. This must be an inward change of the essential elements of our lives and not a mere outward change. Many have gone through the outward identification with churchianity and confused it with Christianity. Christianity is an inward change—a transformation.

Paul says that we are to "be transformed by the renewing" of our minds (*see* Romans 12:2). The word *transformed* means the "changing of the essential element or characteristic." This same word is used of Jesus at the mount of Transfiguration when He was transforming from an earthly body to a heavenly one. His essential nature was changed. So we are told that we must allow God to completely change our inward nature.

God alone can bring such a change. He is the source and the power for it. New Year's resolutions usually become midyear disillusions. Our best intentions fall prey to our worst habits and weaknesses. But when God invades our lives, we can't help but change. It is as though I were to take my key ring and while holding onto it, insert one of the keys into an electrical outlet. There would be change in my life! In the same way, when God is given control in our daily living, there is an inevitable change.

But how does this happen? It happens by the "renewing of the mind." The word *renewing* in the original is *kainos.* It means to be new in nature. It is the same idea Paul referred to in 2 Corinthians 5:17 when he said, "If anyone is in Christ, he is a new creation; the old has gone, the new has come!" God must be allowed to change us completely on the inside so the outward action may be in line with His design for our lives.

Second Corinthians 3:7–18 gives us some helpful insight into this "transforming" and "renewing." Verse 18 tells us we are being transformed into the likeness of Christ by the work of the Lord within our lives. But how do we come to know the Lord and experience Him daily? That answer is given in John 14:21. There Christ says, "Whoever has my commands and obeys them, he is the one who loves me. He who loves me will be loved by my Father, and I too will love him and show myself to him." It is as we are obedient to God's Word that He regularly and freshly reveals Himself to us. Therefore, it is through His commands, as found in His Word, that we see Him.

It is much like looking into a mirror. As we gaze into the Word of God, there is a twofold reflection. First it reflects our own lives and shows us areas that need attention. These are the areas we must allow God's Word to speak to and, therefore, change. But it also reflects the character of Jesus Christ. It is experiencing His character that begins to impact our lives. As we allow that character to permeate our lives, it also shapes our own character and thus we are transformed. But remember, the transformation comes by the "renewing" of our minds. And we can become renewed only as we fill our minds with new material—the Word of God. How are you doing in this area?

The Result of Commitment

The result of such a commitment as has been described thus far is a life that is bent on living out God's will. Biblical directives and promises set forth 95 percent of God's will. The other 5 percent is found by the spiritual discernment which God gives through His Word, prayer, and the counsel of mature Christians. Being what God desires us to be allows us to learn what He wants us to do.

Paul says that the result of this type of commitment is that we will be able to "test and approve what God's will is—his good, pleasing and perfect will" (Romans 12:2). Is he talking here of some mysterious, unknown "will" for our individual lives? I don't believe so. I think he is talking about God's will for our character—His moral will. For it is that will which changes our lives and makes life good, pleasing, and perfect. "But where do you find that?" you are asking. Well, as usual, we often stop short of real answers. Romans 12:1, 2 are quoted and requoted. But I wonder why people don't continue past verse 2. If you take time to read Romans 12:3–15:7, you'll find that it deals with God's will for our character. In verse after verse it gives us direction in living our lives according to God's will. If we were to implement what is found in these verses, we would find a radical change in our daily living. Just a few of the things we would find are:

How to relate to other Christians.

How to really love other people.

How to respond to those who are not nice to us.

How to deal with authority in our work and lives.

How to deal with the importance of our influence on other people.

If we acted on just these areas, can you imagine the difference it would make in our own lives as well as our families, work places, and church!

But it seems at times as we discuss God's will for our lives, many of us tend to balk. We are not sure that following it will bring that which is best. We are afraid that God may call us to give up everything we have and go to deepest, darkest Africa to be a celibate missionary. I am not quite sure why we try to box God by those types of thought processes.

Perhaps the thing we must remember is that there's an entirely different view of God's will when you are standing in it as opposed to standing outside of it. T. B. Maston says it well:

Have you ever approached an old church building with huge stained-glass windows? Those windows appeared dirty, dingy and unattractive. But when you went into the church and looked at those same windows from the inside, you saw their majesty, their beauty, their reverent symbolism. One view was from the outside, the other, inside. This is a rather feeble illustration of the child of God and the will of God. His will frequently looks entirely different, once we are on the inside.[6]

I'll guarantee you'll find the same to be true.

Though Christ had not yet come, Joseph realized that God had done great things on his behalf. The basis of his commitment to the living God was God's repeated provision in his life. Joseph also remembered a God-given dream of destiny that he knew would one day be fulfilled.

He intuitively grasped the character that commitment calls for. Joseph knew that the commitment of his father to God could not substitute for his own dedication. He had to dedicate himself voluntarily to follow God's direction in his own life.

He also realized that God was not looking for a partial commitment. Partial commitment would never have seen Joseph through the trials and tribulations in which he walked. His commitment had to be much deeper in order to anchor him through the difficulties of life. Joseph's roots were deep into God.

Unlike him, we often have shallow roots. When our desert experiences occur, our roots are too shallow or the soil in which we are planted is poor. Perhaps that's why the Bible stresses the importance of being "rooted and grounded" and "built up" in God.

Conformity did not characterize Joseph either. For if that were the case, he would have given in to Potiphar's wife. Instead he was committed to stand strong against the current. Though some of the signposts were down in the society in which he lived, he knew where he was going. He was going to make sure he was standing in the flow of God's will regardless of where the directional signs pointed. He would not be sidetracked from living in the flow of God's will. Instead he was allowing God to transform his life to become the man God had created him to be.

The result of that commitment speaks for itself. Joseph impacted an entire nation. Who are you impacting because of the difference your life exhibits? It may never be a nation but what about your own home? Your work place? Your neighborhood?

You and I can make a difference, as long as we are moving in the flow of God's will.

POINTS TO PONDER

MOVING IN THE FLOW OF GOD'S WILL

1. Explain the relationship between "being" and "doing" in the Christian life.
2. Summarize in your own words the significance of the burnt offering. How does it provide the probable background for Romans 12:1, 2?
3. Recall the description of Robert Boyd Munger's *My Heart, Christ's Home.* Using paper and pen, diagram your own life as though it were a house. Who has control of each room—you or Christ? Are there areas of your house (life) to which Christ has not had access recently? Why?
4. Look up Psalms 51:10
        Isaiah 40:31
        2 Corinthians 4:16
        Colossians 3:10
        Titus 3:5
   What do these teach about being spiritually renewed?
5. Get a commentary and read about Romans 12:1, 2. Outline a plan in which you could explain to another person practical steps in standing in God's will.

11
Big Enough
to Forgive
and Forget

MAXIM:

To err is human, to forgive, divine—
to forgive and forget is supernatural.

"Love means never having to say you're sorry." We heard it espoused in the best-selling book and smash movie *Love Story*. It assumed that in a relationship, the words *I'm sorry* should never be a necessity. Forgiveness should just happen. There should be no special initiative on the part of either party.

It made for a great book and enjoyable movie. Unfortunately, it is unworkable in the reality of daily living.

Most of us remember an event, or events, when our love was shattered or hurt by another. Our emotional world collapsed. Often the resultant hurt was felt to be undeserved and unjust. For many of us the memory of these hurts paints a bitter past, clouds the present, and shackles the future. But how can it be dealt with? Forgiveness is the only workable answer. Forgiveness allows us the miraculous experience of clearing the slate. It is the very act by which ruptured relationships can be restored, wounded feelings healed, and true freedom in living regained.

When I was in high school, I worked in a ladies' shoe store. The experience I gained in serving people as a salesman has proven invaluable. My introduction into the business world was very stimulating. Most importantly, I learned a lot about life. Each evening after the store had closed, we would open the cash register and pull the long tape with the day's account. We would check the tape carefully, mark it, and then file it away in its proper receptacle. An adjustment was then made on the tape left in the register. In doing so we cleared the cash register of all accounts so that we could begin with a new account the following morning.

Forgiveness is like that. We, also, need to clear our mental register of accounts. Bad feelings, attitudes, resentment, and anger need to be withdrawn and put away. It makes all the difference in the world in starting fresh the next day.

Joseph found that to be true as well. After he had been made the prime minister of Egypt, he married a young lady by the name of Asenath. They had two sons, Manasseh and Ephraim. In biblical history names meant a great deal more than they do in our time. They said something significant about the person or circumstances. So it was in this case. *Manasseh* means "to forget." Joseph gave his reasoning for the name when he said, ". . . It is because God has made me forget all my trouble and all my father's household" (Genesis 41:51). As if in concert, the name Ephraim carries a great significance as well. It means "twice fruitful." Again, Joseph explains, "... It is because God has made me fruitful in the land of my suffering" (41:52).

Joseph could never have forgotten if he had not forgiven. Forgetting and forgiving go hand in hand. As with a lock and key, both are indispensable; so it is with forgiveness and forgetting. Significantly, it was only after these two actions that Joseph could rejoice in his blessings in life. What a great lesson for us!

Forgetting False Forgiveness

There are a number of false assumptions about the meaning of forgiveness. They allow us to rationalize our action or inaction instead of motivating us to pursue genuine forgiveness. What are some of these?

Forgiveness is not toleration. Quite often it is easy to excuse ourselves from having to deal with forgiveness. Instead, we determine to tolerate the person who has offended us in some way. We put on a false mask and wince a smile when they enter the room. We coldly acknowledge their presence. Secretly we are praying that they will leave as quickly as possible. There is no love lost when we are with them.

Toleration allows a relationship to stay on a superficial level. Meaningful reconciliation is avoided and quite often ignored. Any remaining friendship is only skin-deep—and sometimes that skin crawls in the presence of each other.

We justify the situation by patting ourselves on the back because we have not totally turned away from the person who has hurt us. Internally we put on our best martyr self-righteousness and convince ourselves that it is all the other person's fault. At the same time, we commend ourselves for not being a snob and utterly ignoring the person on one hand or ruthlessly desiring revenge on the other. We are convinced we are going the "second mile" just to put up with the person and not make matters worse.

Unfortunately no meaningful resolution of the conflict can occur. Things are at best a stalemate. More often than not, the relationship continues to degenerate and wounded feelings become abscesses.

Forgiveness is not ignoring the problem. Others deal with forgiveness by totally ignoring the conflict. They pretend that nothing ever happened. In their mind to acknowledge the conflict would be a sign of weakness. They are not about to be weak so they develop a defense mechanism to cope with the situation instead.

If the other party is totally insensitive or doesn't care, this reaction may not damage their relationship any more than it already has been. Needless to say, however, again there are no steps being made toward a reconciling of the two parties involved. No problem ever goes away because it is ignored. Instead what usually happens is that it gets larger. So it is in conflictual relationships. Most of us hate to be ignored. And when it occurs, the offended party begins to plot strategies on how to get attention or action of some kind.

Forgiveness is not mere words. Words are cheap. Many are said every day with little or no meaning behind them. They are one of the cheapest rates of exchange that can be given in the economy of human relationships. To merely say, "I'm sorry" or "You are forgiven" does not necessarily change anything.

Instead, forgiveness is much more a matter of the will than it is of the word. Granted, words are what most often express forgiveness. But delete the will from behind the words, and you have a hollow, meaningless exchange of verbiage.

To experience true forgiveness, there must be a moral decision of the will to bring the hurt in a relationship to an end. Webster's defines it: "Give up resentment against or the desire to punish; to stop being angry with; to pardon." So if I am to forgive, I must let go of my resentment, bitterness, hurt, and pride. In my will I must make a decision that I desire to make the relationship right more than I desire to feel that I am "in the right" regardless of the status of the relationship. I determine not to allow myself to rationalize away my fault in the difficulty. The fact that it always "takes two to tango" is faced with realism.

God Sets the Example

One of the things I love about the Bible is that it is always very clear both in command and example. God never expects us to do anything He has not already done Himself. In this difficult area of forgiveness, God has offered the most relevant example. He has forgiven you and me.

As we've seen in earlier chapters, we are by our sinful nature out of a right relationship with God until we accept His forgiveness. It is His offer and our acceptance of forgiveness that salvages an otherwise alienated relationship.

If anybody knew that, David did. Following his tragic relationship with Bathsheba, it took him some time to experience reconciliation with God. Many scholars say it took as long as a year. But God was always ready and willing to grant forgiveness. And when received, David exclaimed what a release of burden it was in his life.

Blessed is he whose transgressions are forgiven, whose sins are covered. Blessed is the man whose sin the Lord does not count against him and in whose spirit is no deceit.

Psalms 32:1, 2

David continues as he states the fact of what occurs when forgiveness is not experienced:

When I kept silent, my bones wasted away through my groaning all day long. For day and night your hand was heavy upon me; my strength was sapped as in the heat of summer.

Psalms 32:3, 4

So it is with all of us. When there is a ruptured relationship, we are miserable inside. When no initiative is taken toward reconciliation, our internal being seems to dry up and blow away. Guilt weighs heavy upon us. It is as though a hand is pressing hard upon our heart and mind. Misery is the state of the day. Due to the fact that so much emotional energy is drained and wasted on guilt and misery, there seems to be no stamina or physical energy to be effective in daily living.

God always stands ready to forgive. In fact He is more ready to forgive than we are to receive that forgiveness. And when He forgives, He forgives completely! In fact, He forgets. The Bible says, "As far as the east is from the west, so far has he removed our transgressions from us" (Psalms 103:12).

The New Testament carries on with the same theme, proclaiming our forgiveness through Jesus Christ. When that forgiveness is accepted by faith, the Bible says that "we have been justified through faith, we have peace with God through our Lord Jesus Christ" (Romans 5:1). It is because of Christ's sacrifice in our place and our acceptance of it that we gain peace with God. Whereas there is enmity between God and us until we accept the gift of eternal life, He offers forgiveness through His Son. When that forgiveness is received and appropriated in our lives by faith, forgiveness is granted. Romans 8 goes on to tell us that once that is a reality in our life, absolutely nothing can ever separate us from the love of God that is in Christ Jesus, our Lord (vv. 37–39).

As for our daily relationship with God, the Bible says there is a key in retaining an intimate fellowship. That key is forgiveness. "If we confess our sins, he is faithful and just and will forgive us our sins and purify us from all unrighteousness" (1 John 1:9). To retain a close fellowship with God through His Son, Jesus Christ, forgiveness must be a daily present reality. That forgiveness is only experienced as it is received into our lives on a daily basis.

God has painted a portrait for us of what forgiveness should be like and how it should be exercised. He gave it to us knowing

that we were capable of returning nothing. That is a true love-
motivated forgiveness. To forgive based on the expectation of
someone doing something for us is totally false forgiveness. Instead we must strive to follow the example God has given—take
the initiative to grant forgiveness with no hidden agenda involved.

God States His Expectation

God's forgiveness is free! It is to be received and enjoyed. It is a
liberating energy in life. It is the gateway to a meaningful relationship with Him but it is also a divine illustration. He expects us in
return to deal with others in similar fashion.

> Be kind and compassionate to one another, forgiving each
> other, just as in Christ God forgave you.
>
> Ephesians 4:32

> Bear with each other and forgive whatever grievances you
> may have against one another. Forgive as the Lord forgave
> you.
>
> Colossians 3:13

> For if you forgive men when they sin against you, your
> heavenly Father will also forgive you. But if you do not for-
> give men their sins, your Father will not forgive your sins.
>
> Matthew 6:14, 15

God leaves little doubt of what He expects from us in relationships. He expects a forgiving attitude to be exhibited. Notice He
says nothing about who is right and who is wrong. He just calls us
to practice forgiveness. That kind of action can be motivated only
by love. By love I do not mean a sentimental, weak, emotional
feeling. Instead, I refer to a determination of the will. For true love

is more of the will than it is of the emotion. Anyone who is married knows that. Love based on emotion has no staying power. Real love is a love that freely gives without expectation of anything in return. This love always has the other's best interest at heart. It is based on the type of love that Paul speaks of:

> Love is patient, love is kind. It does not envy, it does not boast, it is not proud. It is not rude, it is not self-seeking, it is not easily angered, it keeps no record of wrongs. Love does not delight in evil but rejoices with the truth. It always protects, always trusts, always hopes, always perseveres. Love never fails. . . .
>
> 1 Corinthians 13:4–8

You and I can only experience that kind of love as God changes our hearts. Once that is allowed, that love must be exercised. Like muscles, it must be used. And God leaves no doubt that He expects it to be used even to the point of forgiveness.

God Sets Forth an Explanation

Hand and hand with His expectation, God explains how we are to put forgiveness into action. He doesn't merely leave it in the theoretical but puts it into concrete practicality. His explanation comes out right smack in the middle of our daily living.

There are basically two cases in which forgiveness must be exercised. One is when we have been wronged. The other is when we have wronged someone. God speaks poignantly to both circumstances in His Word.

When we have been wronged. Peter was constantly trying to be in the spotlight. He wanted to look good. His desire was always to have the right answer. At one point when he was feeling especially spiritual, he asked Jesus how often we are to forgive others. He hinted that to forgive somebody as many as seven times would put us in the "supergood" category. This is based on the fact that rabbinic law at that time required that a person be forgiven three times.

With no hesitation, Jesus popped Peter's spiritual bubble. He answered:

I tell you, not seven times, but seventy-seven times.

Therefore, the kingdom of heaven is like a king who wanted to settle accounts with his servants. As he began the settlement, a man who owed him ten thousand talents was brought to him. Since he was not able to pay, the master ordered that he and his wife and his children and all that he had be sold to repay the debt.

The servant fell on his knees before him. "Be patient with me," he begged, "and I will pay back everything." The servant's master took pity on him, canceled the debt and let him go.

But when that servant went out, he found one of his fellow servants who owed him a hundred denarii. He grabbed him and began to choke him. "Pay back what you owe me!" he demanded.

His fellow servant fell to his knees and begged him, "Be patient with me, and I will pay you back."

But he refused. Instead, he went off and had the man thrown into prison until he could pay the debt. When the other servants saw what had happened, they were greatly distressed and went and told their master everything that had happened.

Then the master called the servant in. "You wicked servant," he said, "I canceled all that debt of yours because you begged me to. Shouldn't you have had mercy on your fellow servant just as I had on you?" In anger his master turned him over to the jailers until he should pay back all he owed.

This is how my heavenly Father will teach each of you unless you forgive your brother from your heart.

Matthew 18:22–35

In the response of the king to the servant, Christ beautifully pictured God's grace and forgiving spirit. He showed that the boundaries of God's forgiveness are inestimable. Regardless of how drastic the breach of relationship, God always stands ready to restore it.

Due to the change in economies, with inflation and deflation, it is hard to determine exactly how much ten thousand talents would equal. Some say as much as ten million dollars. Whatever the case, we know for sure that it would have been several million dollars. Regardless, the king (God) stood ready to pardon.

The pardoned servant, on the other hand, was owed only a few dollars. If we just take it on the basis of the worth of a "talent," we find that the amount owed to the servant would have been only 1/600,000 the amount he in turn had owed to the king. God challenges us to remember His mercy and forgiveness to us. In turn, He expects us to show the same attitude toward those who wrong us. If we fail to do so, the result will be disastrous. The Scripture says that the unforgiving servant was handed over to the "jailers until he should pay back all he owed." How true it is that an unforgiving spirit puts us in our own jail. Anger shuts us up in an emotional stew. As physicians have shown, our physical body reacts negatively when anger is harbored within. Such common ailments as high blood pressure, ulcers, spastic colon, and migraine headaches are often stimulated by a physical reaction to an unforgiving spirit.

Bitterness incarcerates us in a self-centered torture chamber. As anger turns inward, bitterness is the result. As it takes deep root in our lives, it becomes much like the root of a large tree. Though it is beneath the surface, it is constantly drawing nourishment. The root of bitterness feeds on our emotional energies and dissipates our strength for daily living. As the stubborn tree root sometimes breaks the adjacent sidewalk, so often the root of bitterness begins to crush our personality and joy. Until is it derooted, its impact upon our life will be devastating.

Perhaps you have been hurt by a family member, friend, or work associate. You hold onto your resentment tenaciously. You have been unwilling to let go. Let me challenge you just a moment. If this is the case, seriously consider taking these very important steps:

1. Remember God's willingness to forgive you.

2. Recall that He expects you to do the same for others.

3. Realize that you have to take the first step toward resolving the conflict.

4. Recognize that it is a matter of your will and not your emotions.

5. Remember that you are not responsible for the other person's reaction—only for your taking the initiative.

6. Recognize that refusal to offer forgiveness places you in the category of a hypocrite.

As the great philosopher René Descartes said, "When anyone has offended me, I try to raise my soul so high that the offense cannot reach it."

When you have offended someone else. One of the things I've learned in counseling is that reality isn't always the key issue. Quite often perceived reality is the most important fact. So it is in relationships. Even at times when we have not meant to offend someone, we inadvertently have. We have known it to be the case by their action or reaction toward us. Often we have one or two responses to such circumstances: (1) we ignore the situation and try to act as though nothing ever happened, or (2) we justify not taking any action to resolve the difficulty by telling ourselves that we weren't really at fault and that the other person's perception of events borders on the ridiculous.

Unfortunately, God doesn't see it the same way. In Matthew 5:23, 24 the Bible sets forth the explanation of what to do in such circumstances:

Therefore, if you are offering your gift at the altar and there remember that your brother has something against you, leave your gift there in front of the altar. First go and be reconciled to your brother; then come and offer your gift.

Notice that in these verses definite blame is never placed. They do not irrevocably indicate that you were in the wrong. Instead, we read that for some reason your brother has something against you. This means it could even be due to the fact that he perceived something you didn't mean. The fact still remains that there is a breach in the relationship.

God puts the burden on our shoulders. He doesn't say wait until your brother gets a better perception of reality. Nor does He say just to pray about it and it will probably get better. In fact, He says that we must go to our brother and attempt to make things right before we even pray (offer our gift at the altar). Without first taking the initiative to right the relationship, our prayers most probably rise no higher than the ceiling. Perhaps you have felt recently that this is the case with your prayers. You just don't seem to be getting through to the Father when you pray. He seems to be a hundred miles away. Could it be that there is an unresolved conflict with someone in your life? Regardless of whether or not you feel you wronged the person, has he perceived that you hurt him?

I can remember an instance in my own life when a very difficult strain came between me and another person. I felt that he had taken advantage of our relationship and exhibited some unjust actions toward me. As a result, I had walked away from the friendship. Months had gone by and the strain had worn on me a great deal. It regularly came to my mind.

While sitting around waiting for him to take the first step toward reconciliaton, I read those verses in Matthew. Though it didn't set well initially, I realized that it was my responsibility to attempt to bridge the gap. During the months of "cold war," our paths had separated and I had lost track of where he was. I began an effort to locate him. After some difficulty I finally found that he had moved to another state. Picking up the phone, I dialed his number and waited with bated breath.

The phone was answered on the other end. I heard his voice. Many emotions raced through my mind and I almost hung up. But I knew I couldn't. I told him why I had called and asked if he would be so kind as to forgive me for allowing the rupture to occur. Immediately I felt a release within my spirit and a freshness come into my life. I realized that forgiveness is my responsibility, not someone else's. In forgiving I was surrendering all claim to payment of anything I felt he might owe. I had also come to realize that for the man or woman of God, forgiveness is not an option, it is a mandate.

So, the writer is correct: "Doing an injury puts you below your enemy; revenging one, makes you even with one; but forgiving sets you above him."

Forgiving Followed by Forgetting

As the years had passed for Joseph, he had been willing to forgive the injustices done to him. He had evidently forgiven his brothers. He had struggled through the forgiveness of Potiphar's wife, and possibly even Potiphar. Perhaps he had also dealt with the forgiveness of Pharaoh's servant who had forgotten Joseph for two years after he, himself, had been released from prison. But not only had Joseph forgiven, he had also forgotten. This is evidenced by the name of his son, Manasseh.

But what did he forget? Did he forget the event? Did he forget the pit? The prison? The false accusations? Dreary day after dreary day in the darkened cell? The answer is a resounding *no!*

Instead Joseph chose to forget the pain associated with the events. Rather than allow it to spoil his present and future, he determined to put the past aside. He understood that the past was done and nothing he could do would change it. What he did have control of, however, was the present and the future . . . and how he handled that could make all the difference in the world.

Paul was saying the same thing in Philippians, 3:13, 14. There he set forth one of the key elements in successful living.

> . . . one thing I do: Forgetting what is behind and straining toward what is ahead, I press on toward the goal to win the prize for which God has called me heavenward in Christ Jesus.

Paul was putting behind him the memory of false accusations, beatings, disappointments, and criticism. He also, of course, was putting behind the successes.

Only after forgiving can we forget. It is in both that we are able to separate the act involved from the person involved. We find the ability and opportunity to love the person while not necessarily loving the act.

If we are not willing to forget, many are the unfortunate outcomes:

Bitterness   animosity, cynicism, and contempt

Malice   desire to see another suffer

Vengeance   a desire to inflict punishment in retaliation

Clamor   to utter or complain insistently and noisily

Slander   false charges of misrepresentation which defame or damage another

All of these reactions race our emotional motors. They spin our wheels, burn up our energy, and get us nowhere. In allowing such reactions to occur, our minds become closed toward reconciliation. This is unfortunate due to the fact that the hardest thing ever to open again is a closed mind. These emotional reactions wear like a pair of dark glasses—they make the whole world look dark.

Donald Grey Barnhouse described it well when he said, "Forgiveness without forgetting is like vultures feeding on a dead carcass—even the breath of prayer smells of the putrid things."[1]

Perhaps an even more current writer has said it just as well. Recently I clipped an Ann Landers column from our paper. The letter was from a woman who had been married some thirty years and assumed she had a faithful husband. Shocked, she had discovered him in an affair. Sleepless nights and buckets of tears later, she asked Ann Landers if she should both forgive and forget. Ann Landers' response could have been put side by side with the scriptural advice we have seen.

Dear D: You must forgive and forget—for YOUR sake, not his. Let the past bury its dead and look ahead to a new and better life. It is there if you want it. I realize this is easier said than done. You will need a lot of counseling to get the rage out. But it will be well worth the time and trouble. The alternative is ultimate self-destruction.[2]

Perhaps as you've read this chapter, someone has come to your mind. Like Joseph, you have circumstances that need to be forgotten. But before they can be forgotten, they must be forgiven. Whether you have been the one offended or the one perceived as the offender, you must take the initiative. Right now, why don't you call that person? Or go get in the car and drive over and visit with him. If nothing else, write him a letter. Remember, the responsibility is yours.

One last thought: One of the few things that doesn't become secondhand through use is forgiveness.

POINTS TO PONDER

BIG ENOUGH TO FORGIVE AND FORGET

1. Memorize Psalms 32:1, 2.
2. Recall God's forgiveness. How did what you read in this chapter concerning God's forgiveness relate to the last chapter's section "The Basis of Commitment"? How are the two connected? Is forgiveness dependent on commitment?
3. Express in your own words steps which should be taken (1) if you have been offended by someone and (2) if you have offended someone.
4. Donald Grey Barnhouse was quoted poignantly in describing the relationship between forgiveness and forgetting. What did he mean when he said, "Even the breath of prayer smells of the putrid thing" when the two are not mutually involved in relationships?
5. Modern men and women seem to treat forgiveness lightly. Why? How has society influenced the tendency?
6. Forgiveness and forgetting are not easy, but necessary. Spend a few minutes discussing some of your experiences that prove this to be true.

12
When Love Has to Be Tough

MAXIM:

Caring enough to love means caring enough to confront.

Like plagues, mad dogs, and major surgery, most of us prefer to avoid it. Sometimes we'll go out of the way to get around it. And sometimes we just ignore it.

On the other hand, some move quickly toward it. They not only embrace it, they pursue it. To them it is a catharsis for emotional fireworks.

What am I talking about? *Confrontation.*

It is not an easy subject with which to deal. To handle it well is not a science, but rather an art. Joseph had tremendous ability to use confrontation without destroying people in the process. Instead, his ultimate goal was their betterment and growth. The amazing thing is that he was even able to combine confrontation with love. The result was a tough love.

A Private Glance

Confrontation with love has long been difficult for me. The models I saw as I grew up seemed to express love at times and confrontation at others. Unfortunately, the two never seemed to coincide well. The love that was seen was often very tender and special. The confrontation, on the other hand, could be filled with anger and explosive emotions. The results were often wounded people and a struggling journey to get back to comfortable love.

However, I never fully appreciated how difficult it is to balance love with confrontation until God blessed me with children of my own—all with quite different personalities, I might add. The Record family consists of a mother and father, two girls and a boy, and thousands (give or take a few) of stuffed animals. It was with Christy, my older daughter, that I began learning the lesson of tough love.

Christy is a go-getter. She is an outstanding athlete and highly motivated. She also tends to be a bit like her father, unfortunately, in that she has a leaning toward perfectionism. Anything she attempts, she wants to be the best. Whether or not she's spent a lot of time working on a skill makes little difference. If she simply has the desire to do it well, she has difficulty understanding why she can't pick it up the first time and perform at a professional level.

With that kind of drive goes a strong-willed temperament. In responding to that temperament as she grew, I found myself dealing with Christy too often with a quick-tempered emotionalism rather than with logical forethought, reproof, and correction. Realizing what was happening, I determined to change this pattern.

I knew the solution. I would become the perfect father like Robert Young on "Father Knows Best" or Dick Van Patten on "Eight Is Enough." My wife recommended that I study a few books. This led me to outstanding writers—Dr. James Dobson and Chuck Swindoll. Both talked about the need for confrontation, even in the midst of a love relationship. They went on to say that once confrontation has been exercised, it must be followed quickly with care and love. It should never be allowed to be the prevailing atmosphere for an elongated period of time.

It wasn't long after my reading that I found myself sitting in the living room of our home. Christy had obviously had a bad day and was being very short in her communication. I asked her to go help her mother in the kitchen. Giving me an extremely belligerent look, she threw down the material she was holding and stomped out of the room. I realized that the time for confrontation had come. I grabbed her arm as she stormed by, and she began to argue with an ever-increasing volume. Soon she was yelling that I was wrong and that I just didn't understand. (I'm still not sure what it was I supposedly didn't understand.)

Realizing that it was time for tough love, I had to practice confrontation. She was confronted with her wrong actions, firmly corrected, and sent to her room for thirty minutes, unable to read, listen to the radio, or practice any other diversion. She was also grounded for the rest of the day.

I returned to the living room to review mentally what had just happened. I relived each segment of the action. Finally I determined that to the best of my knowledge, I had done exactly what needed to be done in the circumstances. I looked at my watch and found that the half hour had passed. Going to the bottom of the stairs, I called Christy down and asked her to come into the living room with me. We sat down on the couch together and I told her that though I had to be firm in my love a bit earlier, I still loved her very, very much. I wanted her to know that the correction and discipline had been done to help her become the best person she could possibly become. Then I put my arm around her and hugged her and she slid over into my lap. It was at that moment, as we snuggled closely with each other, that I realized fully that confrontation can be characterized by both love and toughness.

The Choice Is Ours

In recent days I've read an outstanding book by David Augsburger entitled *Caring Enough to Confront*. In it he offers the suggestion that confrontation can often be a win-lose proposition. He encourages the reader to seek a win-win opportunity. Rather than the word *confronting*, he offers a new term: "care-fronting."[1] In this approach he encourages us to deal with the issue at hand using maximum information in an atmosphere which produces minimum threat and stress.

He goes on to say there are basically five options we have when confrontation is called for. They are:

1. **"I'll get him."** This approach is definitely a win-lose. It assumes that the one confronting is always right and the one confronted always wrong. There is no middle ground.

2. **"I'll get out."** This approach is taken by the one who is always made uncomfortable by conflict. Withdrawal is seen as the answer. This position proves that silence is not always golden, but sometimes yellow.

3. **"I'll give in."** This is the approach often taken by easygoing personalities. They always want to be nice and never cause waves. This position says that anything should be sacrificed as long as a comfortable rela-

tionship is always maintained. Often hidden by this posture is a tense and frustrated inner being.

4. **"I'll meet you halfway."**   This position assumes that each party involved only has half the truth. The whole truth cannot be known unless the view of both sides is incorporated into the solution. Whether facts are right or wrong pales into secondary significance. This is the ultimate exaggeration of compromise. Unfortunately, if each has only half of the truth, this position may end up with nothing but half-truths.

5. **"I care enough to confront."**   This position desires the relationship to be honest and characterized by integrity. Conflict is seen as both neutral and natural and a potential springboard for improving the relationship.[2]

I believe this latter stance is the position Joseph took with his brothers.

Confrontation at Its Best

It had been twenty years since Joseph had seen his brothers. Their last shared experience was when they had sold him into slavery. They then reported to Jacob, their father, that Joseph had been killed by wild animals. Thus he disappeared from their lives and they attempted to put the memory aside. But what goes around comes around. Now, years later they would meet once more.

The famine touched not only Egypt but Canaan as well. Knowing that Egypt had been on an outstanding food stockpiling program, Jacob sent his sons, less Benjamin (the youngest), to Egypt to seek food. As they arrived, they found themselves before the governor of the land, for it was he who was dispensing and selling the grain. Little did they realize that it was Joseph, their brother.

They were bearded and spoke their native language. On the other hand, Joseph was clean shaven, spoke Egyptian, and wore Egyptian garments and headdress.

Yet Joseph recognized them immediately. Can you imagine what went through his mind? How often when we come face-to-face with people who have wronged us do we find it easy to desire vindication. Now Joseph was faced with the perfect opportunity. His brothers were at his mercy. He could immediately order their death. Or he could dangle them like puppets on a string, torturing them to repay for all the years of difficulty he had walked through. Instead he cared enough to employ confrontation in love. In doing so, he sought to check their attitudes. What was in their hearts and minds? Had they changed since the days they had been so ruthless to him?

We pick up the story in Genesis 42. As Joseph questioned his brothers about their point of origin, they answered that their home was Canaan. Immediately he accused them of being spies who had come to see where Egypt was unprotected. Unnerved, his brothers began to panic. As men who were used to being in control, they found themselves at the mercy of another. Things had quickly gone out of their hands. To the accusations they replied:

> Your servants were twelve brothers, the sons of one man, who lives in the land of Canaan. The youngest is now with our father, and one is no more.
>
> Genesis 42:13

With that Joseph knew a great deal. The brothers still had guilt concerning their mistreatment of him. It had just risen to the surface and they had admitted that one of the original brothers no longer was alive. Obviously they had struggled to some extent with this burden through the years. But further, Joseph also knew that Jacob's love had shifted to young Benjamin in his absence. Jacob had kept Benjamin home to protect him. To his knowledge

Jacob had lost his favorite son, Joseph, and he was making sure it would not happen again. Joseph threw the brothers in prison for three days. He ordered that one of them must return to their father at the end of the three days and bring the youngest brother. Failure to do so would be an admission that they were indeed spies. This would cost them their lives. During this testing, their guilt surfaced once more:

> They said to one another, "Surely we are being punished because of our brother. We saw how distressed he was when he pleaded with us for his life, but we would not listen; that's why this distress has come upon us."
> Reuben replied, "Didn't I tell you not to sin against the boy? But you wouldn't listen! Now we must give an accounting for his blood."
>
> Genesis 42:21, 22

A point of interest was that the brothers had no idea that Joseph could understand what they were saying. He used an interpreter to talk with them so as not to let them know he was conversant in their native tongue. When he heard them struggling with their guilt, he turned and broke down weeping. To cover his reaction, he had Simeon taken and put into prison while the others were ordered to return for young Benjamin. Each was given a bag of grain for his journey. The silver which they had paid for the grain was secretly slipped back into their bags. Unsuspecting, they set out on the return trip.

On the first night's stop, the brothers opened their food bags. In the grain they found the silver which had been paid to Joseph. Though innocent, they realized it would look as though they had stolen the money and dealt fraudulently with the government of Egypt. The Scripture says their hearts sank and they asked, ". . . What is this that God has done to us?" (Genesis 42:28.) Joseph's confrontation had forced them to bring God back into their lives. They were once again seeing the spiritual dimension in life. This is something that all of us must see. It was that spiritual dimension which had stirred their seared consciences of past wrong.

God does that in all of our lives. He seeks to bring people and circumstances across our paths that will force us to deal with unconfessed wrong. The brothers were experiencing firsthand what Scripture means when it says, "Be sure your sin will find you out" (*see* Numbers 32:23). David would say later, ". . . .My sin is always before me" (Psalms 51:3). Indeed, past wrongs are relentless hounds; we can never escape until we deal with them.

When the brothers returned home, they reported the events to their father, Jacob, as they had occurred. Jacob was distraught. He accused them of already depriving him of two of his sons, Joseph and Simeon. Staunchly, he refused to allow Benjamin to go. But Reuben, the levelheaded second oldest, stepped in and took responsibility. Preparing gifts and taking double the amount of silver, the brothers set out on their return to Egypt with young Benjamin.

Scripture says that when Joseph saw them returning, he told his steward to prepare a great feast. Rather than being thrilled, the brothers were terrified. They feared Joseph was trying to lull them into a false security only to accuse them of robbery and inflict punishment upon them. Quickly, they confessed to finding the silver on their return home.

With that, Joseph knew his initial confrontation had worked. God was sensitizing their consciences. Their confession had not been delayed or hidden. Instead they had dealt with it quickly, openly, and honestly. It was evident that God was at work in their lives. They were once again becoming sensitive to the vertical dimension of living. This had been one of the goals of Joseph's confrontation.

As the men were seated for the banquet, to their amazement, they found themselves placed in the exact order of their ages.

Surely questioning looks flew from one to the other. When the food was served, Benjamin's was five times as much as the others. Suddenly, the relational test was put in place. Again Joseph cared enough to confront them with their treatment of others. In giving Benjamin, the youngest, such an overabundance, Joseph invited the other brothers' jealousy. Was their old self-centeredness still in control? Would they resent Benjamin because of the favored treatment? Would they complain and murmur about unfair treatment? When they failed to do so, Joseph must have sighed with relief.

But he was not done yet. As he sent them on their way the next day, as found in Genesis 44:1, 2, one final confrontation would take place.

> Now Joseph gave these instructions to the steward of his house: "Fill the men's sacks with as much food as they can carry, and put each man's silver in the mouth of his sack. Then put my cup, the silver one, in the mouth of the youngest one's sack, along with the silver for his grain."

No sooner had they left than Joseph sent his steward in hot pursuit. When he caught up with them, he accused them of having been treated well only to respond with theft. Unaware of the facts, the brothers vehemently denied the accusations. When they challenged the steward to open any of the sacks, they were shocked at the results. In each man's sack was his silver. In Benjamin's sack was not only the silver but also the silver cup. They had sworn that it would not be in any of their sacks. If it were found, the guilty party should return as a slave of Joseph. Can you imagine how their hearts sank when they saw the cup in Benjamin's sack? What would their father do? They had sworn that they would protect him and return safely with him. And now their lives were falling apart at the seams.

Returning to the city, they found themselves ushered into audience with Joseph. Judah stepped forth responding to the accusations: "... What can we say? How can we prove our innocence? God has uncovered your servants' guilt ..." (v. 16). Once again they acknowledged God's sovereign hand shaping and molding their circumstances. Judah stepped forth with an impassioned plea on Benjamin's behalf. He even offered himself to serve in slavery in Benjamin's place. Finally the emotional impact of the confrontation became so strong that Joseph began to lose control. He sent everyone away—except his brothers. Pulling them closely around him, he said, "I am Joseph!" Can you hear the pin drop? Imagine the terrified silence that his brothers experienced. Time must have seemed to stand still with breathless amazement.

Pulling them even closer, Joseph continued:

> ... I am your brother Joseph, the one you sold into Egypt! And now, do not be distressed and do not be angry with yourselves for selling me here, because it was to save lives that God sent me ahead of you. For two years now there has been famine in the land, and for the next five years there will not be plowing and reaping. But God sent me ahead of you to preserve for you a remnant on earth and to save your lives by a great deliverance.
>
> Genesis 45:4–7

Reunions have to be one of the greatest experiences in a lifetime. That's why we look forward with anticipation to being reunited with loved ones whom we've not been able to see for some time. There is a warmth that pervades our being that only close relationships can bring. Unmitigated joy is experienced in those warm embraces that characterize reunion. Tears flow. Mouths turn upward in brilliant smiles. Hearts beat rapidly. Periods of separation seem suddenly to disappear into a forgotten past. So it was with Joseph and his brothers. As they reached out and touched, the years faded into insignificance. Relationships were born anew. Most importantly, the confrontation had helped reestablish in his brothers' lives the spiritual dimension as well as the relational dimension of living.

The Requirement of Repentance

When legitimate confrontation occurs, repentance is usually experienced in some degree. This was evidenced in Joseph's family. His brothers realized that their past had to be dealt with. Perhaps they had often thought that but had put it off. Many of us do the same. We look for a more convenient season to deal with repenting of past wrong. When confronted, we try to deny our guilt rather than deal with the issue.

Thank goodness Joseph's brothers stepped up to repentance. In doing so they painted an outstanding example for all of us. Scripture is replete with the call to deal with our wrong:

> **"If you repent, I will restore you . . ."**   (Jeremiah 15:19).

> **". . . Repent and live!"**   (Ezekiel 18:32).

> **"Repent, then, and turn to God . . ."**   (Acts 3:19).

One further word in dealing with repentance. I've found in life there is both a true and a false repentance. I experienced the false repentance in college. Often many of the guys in my dorm would party on weekends. On Monday morning, when their heads felt like they would fall off or explode momentarily, there was great repentance. When their bodies just couldn't seem to move except in slow motion, repentance always quickly followed. But their repentance didn't seem to do much good. Witness the fact that the next weekend they would repeat what they had repented on Monday.

That's what Scripture means when it says, "Godly sorrow

brings repentance that leads to salvation and leaves no regret, but wordly sorrow brings death" (2 Corinthians 7:10). Sorrow that is only on the surface will not make a change in one's life. It is shallow and for appearances only. The sorrow is centered more on the consequences than on the act itself.

Godly sorrow, on the other hand, begins in the innermost part of one's heart. It is sorrow based primarily on the wrong and not merely its consequences. True repentance understands that a change must take place. It also understands that wrongs must be corrected. Relationships must be restored. Godly sorrow brings remorse because it recognizes God has been offended.

Obviously, Joseph's confrontation with his brothers via his testing brought true repentance. True confrontation is like that. It always brings a maturing of those involved. Howard Clinebell, well-known counselor, has indicated that confrontation combined with caring brings growth just as surely as judgment and grace lead to salvation.

Confronting With Care

So how does one confront while still caring? It is one thing to read about it. It's another thing to do it. It will never be easy, but at times it will be necessary.

I believe there are some guidelines that will help in confronting with care:

1. *Always confront from a win-win perspective.* This approach avoids win-lose conflicts. We have adopted the perspective of always expecting the best outcome, both in our lives and in the lives of those with whom we are dealing. This type of confrontation invites another to change but does not make it a necessity. The continuation of a relationship is not contingent on a change in the person being confronted. This approach is definitely reflected in Joseph's confrontation with his brothers by the tests he put them through.

2. *Make sure you care before you confront.* Caring should always

precede confronting. It is only when concern for the other person is present that confronting can become "care-fronting." That means we must genuinely care for the other person and be concerned about how the confrontation affects him or her. This will aid us in approaching confrontation from a positive perspective. It will most probably allow us to communicate several positive points before the issue of confrontation is set forth.

3. *Choose with care the words you use.* In constructive confrontation, phrases like "you never" and "you always" should be avoided at all costs. Rarely are these generalizations true. More often they are overstatements employed to drive a point home to gain the advantage. Rather than giving advantage, they fuel the fire of disagreement.

We should also choose with care the construction of our sentences. Denis Waitley, in his excellent book *Seeds of Greatness*, gives some good examples as to how words can make all the difference in the world:

Bad: "You're a liar!"

Better: "That statement doesn't match my inputs; let's check it out together."

Bad: "Your supervisor reports that you're lazy and unproductive."

Better: "Your supervisor and I believe that you're capable of a higher level of output. If I can be of any help, that's my job."

Bad: "Clean up your room, you pigs!"

Better: "All of the bedrooms in our home are neat and clean. While you're cleaning up your room, I'll be at the store. When I get back, I'll show you a way to help separate your clothes better. . . ."[3]

Measure your words well so that you won't have to eat so many of them later.

4. *Raise issues, not voices.* When confrontation takes place, stick to the issue at hand. Stick to the facts and not emotions. Ventilating emotions causes us to use words in confrontation like, "You make me. . . ." Instead of placing the blame on the other person's shoulders, a better approach would be to say, "When this happened, I felt. . . ." This keeps accusations out of the confrontation. Too often emotions begin to take control in confrontation because we have saved up emotional IOUs. Rather than dealing with confrontation when it should have been done, we let things build. Molehills become mountains. It is like a volcano when these mountains explode. By sticking with the issue unemotionally, we do not bring in old baggage. We also do not bring in unrelated experiences or references. We deal with the issue at hand. Sticking with the issue allows us to attack the problem and not each other.

5. *Avoid angry demands.* Anger is natural. It tends to surface at points of confrontation. If it is given in to it may provide emotional release but quite often will rupture relationships. But Scripture gives wise counsel when it says, ". . . Everyone should be quick to listen, slow to speak and slow to become angry" (James 1:19). Again, God's Word warns, "A patient man has great understanding, but a quick-tempered man displays folly" (Proverbs 14:29).

Anger must definitely be controlled. If it is repressed and we pretend it is not there, we are less than honest concerning the situation at hand. However, just as dangerous is the rationalization that we must let it go and "get things off our chest." Remember, you and I are responsible for our emotional reactions toward other people.

Rule your anger or it will rule you. If it has the controlling interest in a situation, it will lead you to make demands in confrontation. The moment that occurs, care no longer characterizes the communication. Rather than coming to an agreed-upon settlement, the one being confronted will tend to "arch his back" and resist any further direction.

Perhaps one of the most helpful thoughts in dealing with confrontation is to ask, "How would Jesus deal with this?" It is obvious that He, like Joseph, did not back down from confrontation when it was needed. He confronted the disciples with their lack of faith. He confronted the money changers in the temple with their incorrect actions and attitudes. He confronted Martha when she was so busy doing things for the Savior that she wasn't taking time to be with the Savior. Yet in each of these instances, love and care characterized His approach. So it was with Joseph. So it can be with you and me.

Tough Love Works

One of my favorite books as an adolescent was Jack London's *White Fang*. You may remember it. White Fang was three-fourths wolf and an outstanding specimen of an animal. In his early years the law that guided his life was simple—survival. The men that controlled his life seemed to be vehicles of anger and hate. White Fang served them only out of fear for his life.

Then one day a kind man by the name of Wheedon Scott became his new master. He was different from the men White Fang had served previously. The love he exhibited reached deep into the heart of the animal and stirred the dormant dog nature.

With each passing day White Fang began to change. A new nature began to develop. Whereas his life to that point had been characterized by fighting, the new quality that began to take over was loving. He yearned to please his new master.

The transformation was beautifully portrayed when White Fang was confronted with a need for change. He had lived so long on the flesh of tender birds that he could not understand what was wrong with killing and eating chickens. Yet his new master confronted him with displeasure. For White Fang it was a cuff on the ear—not a devastating blow, but one that indicated displeasure. It hurt his heart more than his body. But because the confrontation was done in love, he responded with change. He wanted more than anything to please his new master. Soon he slept in the middle of the chicken yard.

The love shared by his new master, even at the point of confrontation, changed the character of White Fang's life. He began to bring every selfish instinct under control. He found in the arena of love and caring a desire to please and to reach his full potential. As a result, his life became better than he had ever dreamed possible.

It is the same with you and me. If we will deal with confrontation in the same way, our lives also will change. If we are being confronted, we must accept criticism and recognize the need for change. Rather than resent the challenge, we should be thankful for it.

And when we need to confront someone else, we should not avoid it but approach it with care. Joseph confronted his brothers and caused them to reevaluate the vertical and horizontal dimensions of their lives. This confrontation changed them! It inevitably brought Joseph and his brothers closer together. Confrontation does not have to be destructive. Instead, when used appropriately, it can be one of the most constructive actions imaginable. Do you care enough to confront?

POINTS TO PONDER

WHEN LOVE HAS TO BE TOUGH

1. Recall the five options we have in confrontation, according to David Augsburger. Which have you practiced? Which do you find easiest? Hardest?
2. Joseph confronted his brothers when possibly it would have been easier to either avoid it or, on the other hand, "really let them have it." Summarize how he handled the situation. What would you have done had you been in Joseph's sandals?
3. Get a Bible dictionary and look up *repentance*. In your own words, what does repentance entail? Outline the difference between "godly sorrow" and "worldly sorrow."
4. Evaluate the guidelines given in this chapter for effective confrontation. Do you agree or disagree? Are there guidelines that need to be added?

13
When It's All Said and Done

MAXIM:

Success is not measured by the things you do but the person you are.

It shouted from newsstands across America in the fall of 1984. Copies were snatched up in quantity. What was it? *U.S. News and World Report's* cover story: "Success. Who Has It? How Do You Get It?" In our drive-for-success society, such a lead story caught the attention of millions.

Success is many things to many people. To some it is an ever elusive phantom. To others it is a fairy tale that happens only to other people. Still others, who have supposedly attained it, flaunt it. In the eyes of most it may be boiled down to four key elements:

wealth, power, position, or prestige. Everyone wants it and some are never satisfied until they get "more." Tony Campolo described it well when he said, "Success is a shining city, a pot of gold at the end of the rainbow. We dream of it as children, we strive for it through our adult lives, and we suffer melancholy in old age if we have not reached it."[1]

I have collected several keen insights concerning this sought-after commodity:

- Success measured merely by money is too cheap.

- You can't reach the top by sitting on your bottom.

- You can't climb the ladder of success with cold feet.

- The ladder of success is full of splinters, most of which you don't notice until you're sliding down the ladder.

- A man in Dallas said, "I spent my life racing up the ladder of success only to find when I reached the top that it was leaning against the wrong wall."

- George Bernard Shaw commented, "There are two great tragedies in life. One is not getting your heart's desire, the other is getting it."

This one really brought a smile to my face:

- A successful man is one who can earn more than his wife can spend.

All of that is well and good but we still don't have any answers. Perhaps we should ask how one gets success. Maybe that will give us a better handle on this elusive dream. There seem to be several different answers, four of which I hear repeatedly:

1. The right conditions. Some people believe that it is a matter of being in the right place at the right time. It sounds so easy. Perhaps that says you are to keep moving until you and success happen to run into each other. It will always be better somewhere else. A change will guarantee a better opportunity. The problems will disappear. Management won't be nearly as shortsighted somewhere else. You will be better understood. Who has not been tempted to bail out using such rationalization?

I will long remember the sage advice of one of the finest philosophers of our day—Charles Schulz. In one of his cartoon clips Schroeder was playing the piano by a hillside while Lucy reclined in the luscious grass. She began to quip, "Just think how much fun everyone on the other side of this hill must be having. They're probably playing and laughing and having a great time. Maybe they're having a picnic or swimming. I'll bet they're having a lot more fun than we are."

For a moment Schroeder continued to tickle the ivories. Finally he looked up and said, "Have you thought that maybe they are saying the same things about us?"

Isn't it true that often we make or break our own opportunities?

2. The right breaks. Others say that the key is having the right breaks. That seems a bit overstated as well. In fact, allow me to introduce someone whose life belies this point.

He had a difficult childhood.

He gained his education under less than ideal circumstances.

He saw his sweetheart die.

He had a nervous breakdown.

He failed in business twice.

He was defeated eight times in bids for public office.

Finally, he was elected president of the United States.

If we were able to ask Abe Lincoln if he thought he got all the right breaks, what do you think he would say?

3. *The right income.* Perhaps the most popular answer is that success means big bucks. After all, that's what enables us to have the accessories which indicate "we've made it."

Television and magazines bombard us with suggestions of things which indicate our success. No ordinary watch will do, only those that reflect "status." Transportation isn't the only consideration in choosing a car. It should add luxury to our ride. And by no means can we forget what we wear. We need a designer's label on our hip, our chest, our shoe, or at least on our tie. A short shopping tour will reveal that these things don't come easily, or cheaply.

But if this is success, why do so many who have so much seem so unhappy? I've always heard that "money may not make you happy, but it will sure get you where the happy people are." I believe if you and I look around we'll find that just doesn't wash. There's more to it than just dollars and cents.

4. *The right looks.* Our world seems to have a hypnotic fixation with good looks. We are influenced to try to look like Robert Redford, Tom Cruise, Linda Evans, or Joan Collins. And if we don't measure up . . . oh well, sorry!

As a result, the cosmetic industry is booming. After we saw the change in Phyllis Diller, we all wanted face-lifts, tummy tucks, and coiffured hair. And some of us still wouldn't be satisfied!

But it isn't just the current media leading the charge. Think of some of your favorite childhood stories. *The Ugly Duckling,* for example. We were taught that his acceptance was based on becoming good-looking. Or how about *Sleeping Beauty?* Have you ever wondered why they didn't name her "Sleeping Average"? More of us would have identified a bit better—well at least I would.

If looks are such a critical ingredient to success, why is it that so many of the "beautiful people" have such ugly lives? Divorce, suicide, and tragedy seem to mark the paths of so many. Looks alone, without a healthy self-image and a vital faith, carry no guarantees of success.

I would like to set forth what I believe to be a more accurate description of success:

> Success is not found primarily in the position you hold, the accomplishments you have attained, or how good you look, but rather in the person you are!

And the person you are is greatly influenced by the attitude you have. In fact, attitudes are the key to successful living.

I've been experiencing the challenge of ground school to learn how to fly. Recently I had a speaking engagement which was not located near a major airport. Since I was on a tight time schedule, it was going to be difficult to make. A friend who was helping me study flying volunteered to fly me in a private plane. So off we went into the wild, blue yonder!

As we flew over South Carolina, I was getting acquainted with the instrumentation in the cockpit. One of the instruments which has always caught my eye is the artificial horizon. Pilots often refer to it as the "attitude indicator." Using a small silhouette of the airplane and a rotating gyroscope, it indicates the relation of the nose of the aircraft to the horizon. When the plane is climbing, it is said to be in a "nose-high attitude." When it is descending, it is in a "nose-down attitude." As we were talking about flying, I couldn't help but think how similar life is. The people I know who handle life successfully are the people who work at having a nose-high attitude. Those who allow themselves to continually slip into nose-down attitudes, inevitably crash and burn.

Another interesting aspect concerning the attitude indicator on an airplane is that it must be set while you are on flat ground. When it is adjusted properly before takeoff, it is said to be on the "zero horizon." The time to standardize this instrument is before you ever get off the ground so that it will be set to show you accurately where your nose is when in the air. This is especially true if you are flying into bad weather.

Life is very much like this too. The time for us to set our attitudes is before we get into the storms of life. If we wait until we are in the center of the turbulence, it is much more difficult to control our attitudes. Instead, the storm usually controls us. As a result, we lose bearing, which sends us into deadly spins.

Viktor Frankl, the great writer who was imprisoned in Nazi Germany, once said, "The last of the human freedoms is to choose one's attitude in any given set of circumstances." Indeed it is a freedom to determine what our attitude toward life will be. Daniel Webster said that attitude is "the manner of acting, feeling or thinking that shows one's disposition." It is by our attitudes that our inner being is revealed. Our attitude toward life, others, and circumstances will always rise to the surface and show us for what we really are.

Your Attitude Toward Life Will Determine Life's Attitude Toward You

Too many today are not satisfied with their lives and always want more. They especially want what others have. The grass-is-greener syndrome lures people away from contentment. But one thing is for sure—if the grass looks greener on the other side of the fence, you can bet the water bill is higher. There is a price being paid which often isn't obvious. All that is seen are the exciting and appealing aspects without any of the difficulties.

One of my friends, a member of our church, is Bobby Jones. Bobby recently retired from the Philadelphia 76ers as an all-pro forward. He played twelve years of professional basketball after playing as an All-American at the University of North Carolina.

More than anyone I know, Bobby exhibits a healthy attitude toward life. He constantly looks for the best in people, not the worst. He always expresses appreciation and gratitude for what he has and does not desire what somebody else has. Most of all, he finds that he gains life at the fullest when he gives his life away to others.

As we were recently discussing our philosophies of life, Bobby shared with me that one of the key maxims of his life has been not to worry about what someone else is doing or not doing. Instead he asks, "What is my relationship with this person and the Lord Jesus Christ? What can I do positively to help the person and to honor the Lord?" Bobby often recalls the incident of Jesus meeting the disciples, following His Resurrection. It is found in John 21. It is the scene in which He expresses love to Peter even though Peter had denied him three times. He challenges Peter three times, in return, to pursue the business that He assigned him. He also tells Peter that He will die a martyr's death. Suddenly Peter catches a glimpse of John and pointing to him quickly questions, "But what about him?" Jesus immediately brings Peter into proper perspective when He replies, "If I want him to remain alive until I return, what is that to you? You must follow me" (v. 22). This story reminds Bobby that we are responsible for ourselves and our attitudes and not those of someone else. We are to be content with where we are and what God is accomplishing in our lives.

Paul summed up the appropriate attitude toward life when he said:

> . . . I have learned to be content whatever the circumstances. I know what it is to be in need, and I know what it is to have plenty. I have learned the secret of being content in any and every situation, whether well fed or hungry, whether living in plenty or in want. I can do everything through him who gives me strength.
>
> Philippians 4:11–13

Thereafter he challenges us to do the same when he says,

> Give thanks in all circumstances, for this is God's will for you in Christ Jesus.
>
> 1 Thessalonians 5:18

That attitude is seen in Joseph's life repeatedly. Regardless of the circumstances, his attitude determined his response. He was content regardless of what was happening around him. Whether in slavery, in jail, or sitting on the throne, he knew God was at work in his life, preparing him to be the best he could possibly be. By an act of his will, he had determined what his attitude would be.

The same is true with you and me. We, not others, determine our own attitude toward life. Yet ironically, our attitude toward life will determine life's attitude toward us.

Our Attitude Toward People Determines Their Attitude Toward Us

My son has always amazed me. Regardless of the time of day, he constantly has a smile on his face. Even though he has to roll out of bed early in the morning to catch the school bus, he comes out buoyant and pleasant. He seems to be able to get out of bed with a smile, saying, "Good morning, Lord!" On the other hand, most of my life I've fallen out of bed and mumbled something like, "Good lord, morning?"

Bryan carries this same attitude toward people. He works at being outgoing and always makes other people feel good about themselves and their circumstances. When we moved to Charlotte, he was four years old. We had not been there more than two weeks when one of the leading men in our church came to me and said he wanted to share an interesting incident about Bryan. Evidently he had met Bryan in the church hallway for the first time and had noticed his broad smile and happy attitude. He approached Bryan to introduce himself, but before he could do so Bryan turned to him and said, "Hi, you look like somebody I'd like to get to know!" He was amazed at Bryan's attitude toward people.

I've watched Bryan for some years now and I think I've found one of the keys to his success with others. He always expects the best from those around him. George Bernard Shaw wrote of the impact of such an attitude in his play *Pygmalion*. The chief character is Eliza Doolittle. She is a flower girl, and everybody treats her just that way. She is seen as a second-rate citizen.

Suddenly, Professor Henry Higgins enters her life. He expects better things for her and from her. He shares his expectations with her and begins to refer to her as a lady rather than a flower girl. Amazingly, Eliza rises to his expectations to become everything he envisioned of her. The result was so well demonstrated in the play that psychologists have now coined a term for this phenomenon, "the Pygmalion Effect." It says that our affirmation of others greatly impacts their development. People grow to fulfill the expectations others have of them. Therefore, it is crucial to have a positive attitude toward those around us.

On the other hand, it has been shown conclusively that criticism and negativism have the opposite effect. David Fink, a psychiatrist for the Veterans Administration, made a revealing study. He witnessed thousands who were "tied up" emotionally and who wanted some type of magical, quick cure for nervousness. As he began to search for such a cure, he identified two main groups: the first group suffered greatly from mental and emotional tension while the second group seemed to be free of such tension.

Gradually one key fact surfaced: Those who suffered from extreme tension had one common trait—they were habitual faultfinders. They constantly criticized the people and things around them. The negative was always easier to find than the positive.

Joseph's attitude toward others throughout his life was characterized by positivism. He sought how he could build up Potiphar, not himself. He didn't elect to get even with Potiphar's wife following the false accusation. Even in prison he looked for ways to help others. Finally, when face-to-face with his brothers in Egypt, he was striving for their best, not his vengeance. As a result, God honored him over and over with the positive response of others toward him. From beginning to end, others played a significant role in his rise from the pit to the pinnacle.

Our Attitude Toward Obstacles Can Turn Them Into Opportunities

Every opportunity presents a difficulty. It is also true that every difficulty presents an opportunity. It is interesting to me as I read the Scripture that every miracle in the Bible started with a problem. Yet God moved into the problems to make them opportunities.

For many of us it seems so much easier to find the difficulties than the possibilities. While working in the business world in Detroit, I had the opportunity to deal with major automotive companies. I heard some outstanding background concerning some of the great leaders in the Big Three. One of them was Charles Kettering at General Motors. A research engineer there told me that when Kettering held an engineers' meeting, he would place a table outside the meeting room with a sign which read, "Leave slide rules here." He did it to discourage the engineers from thinking in concrete terms in the meetings. He wanted to stretch their vision and their imagination. His fear was that if they had slide rules handy, they would reach for them, do some quick calculations, and say, "Boss, you can't do it. It's impossible."

I also had the joy of working with some of the major aircraft companies. Of all the men in these companies, the stories of Igor Sikorsky caught my attention most. When he was twelve years old, he heard it had been proven that human flight was impossible. Yet he went on to build the first helicopter. In his office at Sikorsky Corporation he posted a sign:

> According to recognized aerotechnical tests, the bumblebee cannot fly because of the shape and weight of his body in relation to the total wing area. The bumblebee doesn't know this, so he goes ahead and flies anyway.

We must come to the point of seeing the opportunities in the midst of the difficulties. The difficulties are obvious to anyone who looks. Only one who truly *sees* will visualize the opportunities. That is why I like Robert Schuller's Possibility Thinker's Creed:

> When faced with a mountain,
> I will not quit!
> I will keep on striving
> Until I climb over.
> Find a pass through,
> Tunnel underneath,
> Or simply stay and turn
> The mountain into a gold mine—
> With God's help![2]

Joseph was a man who saw things as they could be. In the midst of all his dilemmas, he was continually aware of God's hand and the opening of opportunities. Patience characterized his willingess to hang tough and persevere in the face of adversity. It was that perseverance and faith in God's sovereignty that led him to the possibilities.

Nowhere in Joseph's life is this attitude better exhibited than in the situation following the death of his father. Fearing that Joseph had been kind to them and provided for them simply due to his love for Jacob, his brothers came before him, fell on their knees, and proclaimed, "We are your slaves." But Joseph with kindness responded:

> Don't be afraid. Am I in the place of God? You intended to harm me, but God intended it for good to accomplish what is now being done, the saving of many lives. So then, don't be afraid. I will provide for you and your children. . . .
>
> Genesis 50:19–21

In spite of all the difficulties, Joseph was still able to say, "God intended it for good." That's the attitude that turns obstacles into opportunities! Can you say that about your present obstacles? If you can't, you'll never see the opportunities.

Your Attitude Toward the Present Will Determine Your Attitude Toward the Future

So many people are waiting—waiting for things to get better, waiting for a new job, waiting for a new move, waiting for the next vacation. The list is lengthy. They feel that something in the future will somehow greatly improve the present. Unfortunately, they have it totally turned around. It is the present that totally changes the future.

I find many people who are waiting for some great opportunity in the days just ahead. They believe when the great opportunity comes, they will rise to meet it and find great success. They will suddenly be infused with power, ability, and intelligence to handle whatever great challenge comes their way. How deluded is this thought process.

All of us must return to the fact that today is the building block for tomorrow. We must strive with excellence in the present so that we will be able to accomplish God's plan for our future. I believe J. D. Rockefeller, Jr., summed it up well when he said, "The secret of success is to do the common things uncommonly well."

How you and I react to today's challenge will determine how we will meet tomorrow's opportunities.

Our friend Joseph displays an outstanding example for us once again. He did not allow himself to be shackled by the disasters or triumphs of the past or sidetracked by the hopes for the future. Instead, he gave his best each day to the matters at hand. At each stage of his life he met his responsibilities with dedication and excellence. He did the common things, even in slavery and in prison, uncommonly well.

How are you performing in your daily routine? Are you doing things which may seem so common, uncommonly well? It is only to those who are faithful in the common things that God brings the bigger possibilities. If we are failing in our present routine, we can be assured that we will not succeed in handling future opportunities and responsibilities. There is nothing more important than what you have before you to do this very day. Tomorrow will take care of itself.

So What About Success?

So indeed, success is the person that you are. You do not have to wait until you attain more things or gain a higher position. Neither is success found in notoriety or surface popularity. Instead, success is found in being the person God designed you to be. It is having the right attitudes. An anonymous poet has summed it up well.

Success is speaking words of praise
In cheering other people's ways.
In doing just the best you can
With every task and every plan.

It's silence when your speech would hurt,
Politeness when your neighbor's curt.

It's deafness when the scandal flows,
And sympathy with others' woes.

It's loyalty when duty calls;
It's courage when disaster falls,
It's patience when the hours are long;
It's found in laughter and in song.

It's in the silent time of prayer,
In happiness and in despair.
In all of life and nothing less,
We find the thing we call success.

But What About Failure?

In our day of success and motivation seminars, it is quickly beginning to sound as if there is no place for failure in life. To be successful, it seems that one must avoid failure. As a result, there are many hypocrites running around. They are trying to give the impression that failure has no part in their lives. It is just one success after another. They are fearful of someone seeing any cracks in their life-style. Even if they are successful on the outside, they feel like failures on the inside. Two psychologists from Georgia State University have labeled this the "Imposter Phenomenon."[3] They find that those who are constantly trying to show the outward form of success often feel like phonies inside. They feel they have "gotten away with it" and fooled many around them. Due to their fear that they will be exposed as fakes, they dread any potential failure that could destroy their plastic image.

This is diametrical to biblical teaching. In God's Word there is always room for failure. In fact, by the world's standards, some of the greatest heroes of Scripture could be discarded as pitiful failures:

<u>Noah had a problem with alcohol.</u>

<u>Rahab was a prostitute.</u>

<u>Abraham had a problem with lying to cover up.</u>

<u>David was a murderer and adulterer.</u>

<u>Moses had a temper problem.</u>

<u>Even Joseph at a young age displayed a bit of an ego problem.</u>

Failures and mistakes are a vital part of effective living. Bobby Jones says that he hated to lose games in his basketball career. Even more, he hated it when he didn't learn anything from losing. Bobby would always strive to learn from his mistakes to become an even better player. As a result, he has one of the very few retired jerseys in the history of the Philadelphia 76ers. Perhaps the biggest mistake is the fear that we will make one. That fear shows our weakness, for often mistakes are the finest tutor we will have in life. Theodore Roosevelt said, "Show me a man who makes no mistakes, and I will show you a man who doesn't do things."

Let me share with you some rather interesting facts that you may not know about some "successful" people:

<u>Babe Ruth struck out more times than any man in baseball's history.</u>

<u>Dr. Seuss's first children's book was rejected by twenty-three publishers: the twenty-fourth publisher sold six million copies.</u>

<u>Reggie Jackson batted .178 his first year in the majors.</u>

<u>Henry Ford went broke at forty.</u>

<u>Walt Disney went broke seven times.</u>

Einstein was four before he talked and seven before he read, and flunked math in school.

The ability to fail is the key to successful living. If a mistake or failure paralyzes us, our attitudes will tend to atrophy. So will our spiritual life. Richard Needham says, "Strong people make as many and as ghastly mistakes as weak people. The difference is that strong people admit them, laugh at them, learn from them. That is how they become strong."[4] Indeed it can be said that the only total mistake is the one in which we learn absolutely nothing. That leads us to the inevitable conclusion that the measure of success is not whether or not we have a tough problem or have made a mistake—the question is if the tough problem or mistake we have now is the same we had last year, last month, or last week. If so, we have misused our mistakes and failures.

Though Scripture does not delineate the mistakes Joseph experienced in his life, we would be less than honest to assume he had none. One key truth we can see from his story, however, is that mistakes never destroyed him. He was able to rise above whatever failures he may have had. Each must have been used as stepping-stones to opportunity. What a challenge he gives to us to do the same.

What Now?

As we've journeyed back through the life of Joseph, we've traveled a long distance. We've seen a great many insights. We've received challenges to change and improve. Throughout the pages in his life, the call rings clear to you and to me not to stay the same as we are now but to strive toward what we can be.

Perhaps as you've read these pages, you have felt as I have when reading. You've laughed some. You have pondered very serious and provoking thoughts. And at other places perhaps you've totally disagreed. But hopefully, throughout, you have experienced the touch of God in your life and in your thought processes. That has often happened to me. But then I take the book, put it on the shelf, and before long it is forgotten. Maybe a few illustrations have been gleaned, but there it seems to have stopped. My hope is that this is not the case with you and this book.

Most probably as we've made this journey together you have had thoughts that you just aren't cut out like Joseph. You don't believe you have all the characteristics that he had. You're not sure you can handle those who have wronged you in the same manner he did. Or perhaps you feel that whatever it is you are waiting for, the wait has just been much too long.

As we wrap up our study together, one of the burning questions must be, "Where do we go from here?" I would like to challenge you to put feet to your faith. Take action to change your attitudes. But how do you do that? I believe the only way is to take one step at a time. The first step is to set down personal goals and objectives which will result in the desired change. Let me define these terms.

A goal is an overarching direction or aim which I desire to achieve. It is rather large in scope and not necessarily measurable.

An objective, on the other hand, is a limited action which is both realistic and measurable. It may require several objectives to reach my ultimate goal.

Let's take these terms and put them into practice. Perhaps as you read the chapter "Big Enough to Forgive and Forget," a ruptured relationship came to mind. In your heart you know you need to act. Your goal would read something like this:

I desire to reconcile the relationship.

But as you can see, that is not measurable. It is also sufficiently vague to allow a lapse into inactivity and not follow through. To that must be added objectives. The objectives might be something like these:

1. I will begin to pray for five minutes daily for the other person and for our reconciliation.

2. I will contact the person within the next two days and arrange a meeting.

3. Before meeting with the person, I will prepare what I want to say during our time together.

4. During the meeting, I will not use any accusatory language but will instead take the initiative and ask for forgiveness on my part.

You may want to go back and review some of the things we discovered in the chapter "Big Enough to Forgive and Forget." For others, there will need to be goals and objectives made for waiting patiently in the midst of present circumstances. For others, it will be coping with and responding to temptation you are presently facing. Some will have been challenged on how to witness better at their place of employment or within the traffic pattern of their daily routines. Whatever the case, we must determine a plan for where we're going and what we're going to do. Remember that the best way to plan to fail is to fail to plan.

Lest you think that making goals and objectives would be presuming on God's hand in your life, please remember that they are nothing but mere statements of faith for the future. They are the seeds of what you believe can be and should be. Jesus Himself said, "Suppose one of you wants to build a tower. Will he not first sit down and estimate the cost to see if he has enough money to complete it? For if he lays the foundation and is not able to finish it, everyone who sees it will ridicule him, saying, 'This fellow began to build and was not able to finish'" (Luke 14:28–30). You cannot count the cost unless you have the goal and the objectives to get there. I challenge you right now to take a pen and paper in hand and begin to establish your goals for changing your life.

When I lived in Texas, there was a favorite story that floated among Texas sportsmen. It concerned Jake, a small-town Texas fisherman. It seems that Jake had an uncanny ability and reputation for catching tremendous numbers of fish. His reputation spread far and wide.

Continually hearing about the exploits of Jake, a federal game warden decided to investigate. Dressed in civilian clothes, he drove to the small southern Texas town and began to inquire about Jake. Several indicated that if he returned at the end of the day they would point Jake out. Sure enough, about sunset, one of the townspeople pointed to a man driving up in a pickup truck.

Strolling over to the pickup, the game warden introduced himself by his name only. He told Jake that he had heard of his reputation and had driven a long way to learn his secret to effective fishing. He inquired if Jake would be willing to teach him his skills. Without hesitation, Jake willingly agreed. He told the warden to meet him at the town square the next morning at 4:30 A.M. From there, they would head out to their fishing adventure.

The next morning the game warden, in his civilian clothes, was picked up by Jake. The boat was attached to the back of the pickup. Off they went through the back fields of Texas on what seemed to be an endless drive. Finally, breaking through some brush, they stopped on a ridge overlooking a beautiful hidden lake.

Backing the boat into the water, Jake took out a small leather satchel and put it into the boat. The warden was interested in the fact that there was no fishing gear anywhere. Deciding not to ask too many questions, he simply got into the boat and rode with Jake to a small isolated cove in the beautiful body of water.

As the motor was shut off, Jake turned and opened the leather satchel. To the game warden's amazement, Jake pulled out a stick of dynamite. Lighting it, he threw it overboard. BOOM! The surface water erupted with a huge explosion. Suddenly stunned fish began to float to the surface. Quietly and without excitement, Jake started his trolling motor and began to move toward the stunned fish, scooping them into the boat with his net. When the boat was full, they traveled back across the lake, put them into the bed of the truck, and iced them down.

This sequence of events happened several times. Finally, shaking himself back to reality, the game warden pulled out his wallet. Showing his identification to Jake, he said, "I apologize, Jake. I must be honest. I am a federal game warden. I also must say that I am absolutely amazed with your creativity and ingenuity. But at the same time when we get back to the other side of the lake, I must put you under arrest for fishing illegally."

Without hesitation, Jake reached down, grabbed another stick of dynamite, and lit it. Handing it to the game warden, he smiled and gently said, "Are you going to sit there and talk, or are you going to fish?" Now the choice is yours. Having traveled through the life of Joseph with me, the question comes down to, "Are you going to talk or are you going to fish?"

I hope you decide to fish—to put into action what you've read. Believe me, it will change your life.

POINTS TO PONDER

WHEN IT'S ALL SAID AND DONE

1. The twentieth century is so fascinated with "success." How do you define that term? Where have you been seeking success?
2. In this chapter a definition of success was set forth:

   Success is not found primarily in the position you hold, the accomplishments you have attained, or how good you look, but rather in the person you are!

   What is your evaluation of this definition?
3. If attitudes are so important, how do you establish them? When wrong attitudes exist toward life, people, obstacles, and the present, how can they be changed?
4. What are many of the common views of failure that are in need of rethinking? What constitutes failure? Is it always negative?
5. Outline at least five goals for your life for the next three months. They may deal with any area discussed in our study. Be sure they are realistic and measurable. Write them down and pray about them daily. Get ready to *watch your life change!*

Epilogue

As Joseph employed the principles we've discovered in his life, God honored him again and again. He was reunited with his family, and relationships were healed. He was able to be present at the death of his father and was able to be of special strength to the entire family in that time of loss.

The Scriptures are fairly quiet concerning the rest of Joseph's life. He lived successfully and happily. No other major traumatic events occurred. God merely honored his faithfulness and his willingness to strive to be all that he had the potential of becoming.

When Joseph died, he was 110 years old. He had seen his children and his great-grandchildren. His last request was to be buried in his homeland—the land of Canaan. But even in death, he was promising those around him that God would surely take care of them and come to their aid. From beginning to end, God was the center of his life. He had indeed learned how to have maximum living in a mad, mad world.

Source Notes

Introduction   Life Can Be the Pits

1. I am indebted to Dr. Charles Feinberg for the term *prefillment*. This is used as the opposite in meaning of *fulfillment*. It means "serving as a picture of what is to come in the future."

Chapter 1   Overcoming a Weak Foundation

1. Dietrich Bonhoeffer, *The Cost of Discipleship* (New York: Macmillan Publishing Co., Inc., 1969), p. 69.

Chapter 3   The Devil Made Me Do It

1. Donald Seibert and William Proctor, *The Ethical Executive* (New York: Simon & Schuster, Inc., 1984), p. 37.

Chapter 4   Who, Me? Handling Unjust Accusations

1. H. D. Spence and T. S. Exell, eds., *The Pulpit Commentary*, vol. 8 (Grand Rapids, Michigan: William B. Eerdmans Publishing Co., 1950), p. 3.

Chapter 7   Witness While You Work

1. Jacob M. Braude, *Speaker's Encyclopedia* (Englewood Cliffs, New Jersey: Prentice-Hall, Inc., 1955), p. 14.

2. Creath Davis, *Sent to Be Vulnerable* (Grand Rapids, Michigan: Zondervan Publishing House, 1973), p. 20.

3. Tom Peters and Nancy Austin, *A Passion for Excellence* (New York: Random House, Inc., 1985), p. 206.

4. Ibid.

Chapter 8   The Indispensable Ingredient

1. Meg Greenfield, *Reader's Digest*, November 1986, pp. 224–227.

2. J. Oswald Sanders, *The Holy Spirit and His Gifts* (Grand Rapids, Michigan: Zondervan Publishing House, n.d.), p. 138.

3. Rene Pache, *The Person and Work of the Holy Spirit* (Chicago: Moody Press, 1954), p. 118.

Chapter 9   The Marks of a True Leader

1. Warren Bennis and Bert Nanus, *Leaders* (New York: Harper & Row Pubs., Inc., 1985), p. 18.

Chapter 10   Moving in the Flow of God's Will

1. William Barclay, *The Letter to the Romans* (Philadelphia: The Westminster Press, 1955), p. 168.

2. Ibid., p. 169.

3. George Arthur Buttrick, ed., *The Interpreter's Bible*, vol. IX (Nashville: Abingdon Press, 1954), p. 581.

4. Robert Boyd Munger, *My Heart: Christ's Home* (pamphlet by Billy Graham Evangelistic Association), p. 12.

5. Paul Tillich, "Do Not Be Conformed," *Twenty Centuries of Great Preaching,* Clyde E. Fant, Jr., William M. Pinson, Jr., eds., vol. X (Waco, Texas: Word, Inc., 1971), p. 82.

6. T. B. Maston, *God's Will in Your Life* (Nashville: Broadman Press, 1964, p. 20.

Chapter 11   Big Enough to Forgive and Forget

1. Donald Grey Barnhouse, *Let Me Illustrate* (Old Tappan, New Jersey: Fleming H. Revell Company, 1967), p. 121.

2. The *Charlotte Observer*, Wednesday, April 24, 1985.

Chapter 12   When Love Has to Be Tough

1. David Augsburger, *Caring Enough to Confront* (Ventura, California: Regal Books, 1983), p. 10.

2. Ibid., pp. 13–15.

3. Denis Waitley, *Seeds of Greatness* (Old Tappan, New Jersey: Fleming H. Revell Company, 1983), p. 33.

Chapter 13   When It's All Said and Done

1. Anthony Campolo, *The Success Fantasy* (Wheaton, Illinois: Victor Books, 1982), p. 9.

2. Robert Schuller, *The Be-Happy Attitudes* (Waco, Texas: Word, Inc., 1985), p. 30.

3. Joan C. Harvey and Cynthia Katz, *If I'm So Successful, Why Do I Feel Like a Fake?* (New York: Simon & Schuster, Inc., 1986), pp. 4, 15.

4. Alan Loy McGinnis, *Bringing Out the Best in People* (Minneapolis, Minnesota: Augsburg Publishing House, 1985), p. 73.